BU
REVELATIONS

By

TOM DAVIES

A road trip into the darkness and light of
Australia

To Christie & Penny,

with regards

Tom Davies.

Wales' most passionate and creative writer – Max Boyce

LLYFRAU
CAMBRIA

Published in the United Kingdom in 2015 by
Cambria Books, Wales, United Kingdom

Cover by Escape to Design

By the same author

FICTION
The Electronic Harvest
One Winter of the Holy Spirit
Black Sunlight
Fire in the Bay
I, Conker
Polly Garter's War
The Tyranny of Ghosts

TRAVEL
Merlyn the Magician and the Pacific Coast Highway
Stained Glass Hours
Landscapes of Glory
The Celtic Heart
Wild Skies and Celtic Paths
The Road to the Stars
Through Fields of Gold

THEOLOGY
The Man of Lawlessness
The Visions of Caradoc

MEMOIR
The Reporter's Tale
Testament

ABOUT THE AUTHOR

Tom Davies, a Welshman born and bred, was a state scholar at University College Cardiff where he graduated in honours philosophy. He has been a seaman on ships around Australia and Africa, a social worker in the Lower East Side of New York and was the first graduate to be sent to Indonesia by Voluntary Service Overseas.

He later trained as a journalist with the Western Mail, the national newspaper of Wales, and went on to work on the Atticus column on The Sunday Times, as a feature writer in the Sunday Telegraph and the Observer where, for three years, he was their diarist Pendennis.

He became a full-time writer in 1983 and has since written eighteen books beginning with Merlyn the Magician and the Pacific Coast Highway, which was shortlisted for the Thomas Cook travel prize and acclaimed by Bono, the front man of U2, as being a book that changed his life. Black Sunlight, his best-selling novel, was set in the 1984 miners' strike and Stained Glass Hours, a pilgrimage narrative, won the Winifred Mary Stanford Prize for the best book with a religious theme.

Davies has also written five travel books about various pilgrimages throughout Europe including those to Compostela and Rome and his latest book is a memoir, The Reporter's Tale.

Married with three sons, he runs an art gallery and lives in Bala in the mountains of Snowdonia, North Wales.

To everyone who has ever believed – or suspected – our media is firmly behind the rise of modern terrorism this book is prayerfully dedicated.

CHAPTERS

1: A Rock 'n' Roll Preparation

This huge Amazonian woman - all ripped shorts and legs that went on for ever – sat down next to me on the Manly ferry and proceeded to rummage in a backpack before producing a giant carrot. This carrot was none too clean but she stuck it in her mouth and bit into it with a big crack. A young girl in the seat in front actually jumped on the first crack and went even higher on the second. In this way the small ship echoed with loud cracks and bulldozer munchings. You have never heard such a racket coming out of one carrot. She was a European backpacker, I guessed. Sydney seemed full of them that year and I'm told they would even eat gravel if they were hungry enough. After she let out a loud belch I decided I could put up with it no longer and, as she produced yet another carrot, I moved away.

The cityscape all around us was seriously and sensually beautiful, the sea riffled by night breezes and, in the distance, the spiky horizon of Sydney skyscrapers with Circular Quay directly in front of us where all my Australian dreams had begun and taken root in my life.

In a definite sense this place is my own private harbour, the beginning and end of all my journeys to Oz. I first came here when I was seventeen, a young and wild cabin boy on a tramp cargo ship, the Canopic, that went on to deliver – and pick up - cargo to most of the main Australian ports. My two sons, Julian and Steffan, came to Sydney in their early twenties. They had just finished their education and, not knowing what to do with their lives, it is no

1

exaggeration to say that Sydney saved them after a few years of drift. My youngest boy, Nathan, came here to live six years ago and has become a successful businessman in Manly.

And what I did not know on this gorgeous night as we chugged towards Circular Quay, on our way to the Opera House and a concert by the great Neil Finn, was that, after a lifelong search, this same country was going to give my work and ideas a meaning and affirmation which up to this point it didn't have.

But first there is a trip around Oz to be made; a journey which was going to last at least a year and already we were negotiating to buy a Winnebago to take us on our way. Liz, my wife, who was 69 today, was going to do the driving because my foot wasn't up to it although I will be in charge of the toilet cassette and petrol tank, it has been decreed, keeping the one empty and the other full.

I was brimming with anxiety about whether I was up to it. At 73 I had become a ball with very little bounce. I'd had two heart operations over the past ten years which had taken a lot of my strength, and a stroke which had left my right hand stiff. And there was something painful called plantar fasciitis in my left foot, an inflammation of the instep ligament which I'd been trying to get rid of, unsuccessfully, for eighteen months. Surely I didn't have long to go 'till I dropped and it might well be in the middle of the Bush miles from anywhere. However, there we were, living in Manly, a seaside suburb of Sydney where we have been sorting out the Winnebago and buying what we needed for the journey. We had no plan or route. We were just going to follow our noses through this land and see what turned up. There was no Plan B.

Neil Finn, formerly of the majestic Crowded House, had long been a big favourite of ours and we were looking forward to the concert as we crossed the convict haunted waters of the bay framing the scallop shapes of the opera house, black on red, as it perched on the end of its famous promontory. This opera house is always thrilling to see and unfailingly lifts the spirits, so full of strength and Aussie confidence. Let no dog bark as I speak my name, it says.

The great curve of Sydney Harbour Bridge hovered over us with people crossing it, hurrying home in the pink sunset and, right across the water, Luna Park funfair, its attractions a bit tatty now, rather like a mini-Disneyland that's lost its way home to Anaheim. Birds wheeled in the darkening sky calling out the good news that Neil Finn was about to go on stage.

Neil Finn, a Kiwi, has a voice unique in its sweetness, as if gargling songbirds. With his new band, Dizzy Heights, tight and driving, they began pouring all those great hits over us – Distant Sun, Don't Dream It's Over and, of course, Weather With You. There was also the marvellous pounding energy of I Got You which had many sections of the audience on their feet and dancing wildly, a song which Finn wrote when he was with his first Kiwi band Split Enz. One of my favourite ever records followed with the lovely abject surrender of Fall at Your Feet which, even after all these years, still brings tears to my eyes.

I get so happy I cry like a baby in rock concerts; it's all I ever do. On reviving hours like this we can prepare ourselves for the pain and loss which comes to us all sooner or later; we are given new strength for any difficult journeys ahead.

I've written a lot over the years about how rock 'n' roll can break your heart and save your life. Certainly it has torn me apart and put me together many times and I'm thinking of one transcendent night sitting at the feet of The Who in a coliseum in Cannes or that endless, inspiring concert by Bruce Springsteen when he first came to London. I still go a bit gaga as I remember the night when Pink Floyd first introduced inflatables in Wembley.

Anything by the Stones always kept me cheerful for at least a fortnight.

Well this concert by Finn and co. was well up there with all of them; a gorgeous outpouring of sound which took us one way and then another before inviting us to join in the same healing communion.

Certainly it seemed to cure many of the ills I've been complaining about as well as giving Liz a birthday treat she will never forget.

Yes, we all came together during that concert with our faith restored in everything by the time it was over. As Pete Townshend once brightly said: "Rock 'n' roll never cured any problems but it sure helps you dance all over them."

Suddenly everything seemed exciting and possible on that sacred Sydney night as the midnight ferry took us back home to Manly. Tugboats pooted past and gulls flew overhead calling out to us to throw them some food. Drunks were fast asleep on the seats all around us although there were no backpackers eating carrots on our way home – or gravel come to that – and I felt my spirit alive with the prayer that, if our battered, strife-torn world will ever again see a religious revival, it will come out of rock 'n' roll.

Few understand the healing power of rock 'n' roll. It brings us together and makes us new again. It gives us hope too and can even fix broken hearts. And, on this blessed Sydney night scattered with stars, it certainly prepared us for the long and possibly dangerous journey we were about to undertake.

2: The Godzilla of the Insect World

We have now been in Sydney for three weeks, anxious to get off around Australia but still sorting out multiple problems with the Winnebago. You name it and it had to be fixed including the reversing camera which insisted on showing the reverse view upside down. Then there was the driving seat which wouldn't adjust and it all came to a head yesterday with a furious argument with the van dealership in which I asked for my money back but predictably got nowhere.

There could of course be lots of worse places to get stuck in than beautiful Manly, one of Sydney's more gorgeous suburbs with wide, tree-lined boulevards, pleasant shops and bars, the harbour on one side and the quietly swelling ocean on the other on which the sun kept glittering like freshly scattered diamonds. The people are the friendliest and most open I have ever met; you might just stand in front of crowded table in a street there, say a few words and they'll rise up in warm and enthusiastic conversation. Having a Welsh accent helps, I guess. No matter where you are people always seem to like the Welsh.

Even the bums who hang out around the Manly pier seem the happiest bunch of bums you'll ever meet. They're all tanned with long bleached hair and cackle a lot as they speak to one another in their own bum language with lots of effing and jeffing. They often catch their own fish for dinner under the pier, competing with the penguins who hang out under there. A few have even got their own skateboards and, if we were ever looking for a solution to the problem of street bums in the UK, we could do no worse than transport the lot of them to Australia where they could start a new sunny life in places like Manly and would all quickly become as happy as small babies. The Aussies might well have an objection or two to that proposal though. They like immigrants who have a bit of money and seem happy to work.

You can often spot the huge black shapes of giant manta rays in the water, not that they worry the Aussies who will simply swim around them and their giant stinging tails. Aussies don't seem to worry about anything that may show up in the sea and the other day a shark turned up in the middle of a surfing competition here. You would think that would be the cue for all of them to scarper straight out of the sea, as in that stampede in Jaws. But oh no. They simply sent out a lifeguard on a jet ski to scare the shark away and carried on surfing.

At night giant fruit bats tumble around the trees and overhead wires in the main street, often causing power cuts and you might be sitting on a balcony eating a baguette when you will be suddenly aware of a row of parrots on the railings in front of you, grumbling impatiently to share in your bread. They have strange calls which they seem to have modelled on the single ascending notes in ET.

But there were a number of other problems we found we would have to deal with, to put it mildly. We had been staying with Nathan and his partner Sally in their flat just on the water in Manly and, as I pulled back the bed sheets to get into my bed one night, I looked up at the wall and right there, looking back at me, was a giant spider the size of a dinner plate: the Godzilla of the insect world. I didn't actually scream, although everyone else swore I did, but I admit to being highly agitated as I rushed back into the living room looking for something big and hard to give this monster – a huntsman, I learned – a big crack on his ugly head. He alone would

6

have scared the battiest of celebrities out of that jungle in one second flat.

But Nathan, who has become completely Aussified since he came here, wasn't having any of that. Huntsmen keep insects down and deserve a life too, he claimed. He would trap him and escort him off the premises so that presumably he could find his way to another bedroom in another building where he could frighten the life out of someone else about to get into bed. Like draughts huntsmen can change their shape and get through the smallest cracks anywhere. But I was far from convinced they deserved a life too.

The huntsman legged it across the wall pursued by Nathan's big plastic beaker and, after several near misses, he finally got him and released him outside. By now my blood had drained into my very toes and, after a few teetotal years, I really could have done with a stiff drink or three to calm me down.

I did resist the call to booze but there was more insect strife to come later that night when, in the grip of my usual four o'clock bout of insomnia, I put on my slippers and went to the kitchen to make myself a soothing cup of tea only to turn the light on and confront two cockroaches the size and colour of Mars Bars sitting together on the tiles discussing whatever cockroaches talk about in the middle of the night. I assumed these creatures didn't enjoy Nathan's rather strange protection and quickly decided to step on them. But I didn't even get close to stepping on either.

They didn't make a mad rush for deep cover under the stove or anything but just seemed to stand there looking up at me to see what I was going to do first. Well I was going to pancake the pair of them flat with my slippered foot that's what I was going to do, but the two of them sold me a dummy, running as if they were going one way before reversing faster than Usain Bolt leaving me stamping on fresh air. I had never seen anything like it since the rugby player Barry John jinked his way through the English line way back in the Sixties.

Well this story has a really stupid end, I admit, since the next morning I bought a hand vacuum cleaner in the local shopping centre with which I was going to suck the roaches up and squirt them out into the garden. Look Nathan, I'm not going to crush them, just suck them up and eject them into the garden because I need to drink tea in the middle of the night when I can't sleep.

It didn't reflect well on my sanity going to make a cup of tea in the middle of the night armed with a vacuum cleaner, I do admit, but, perhaps fortunately for everyone concerned, the two cockroaches seemed to have got the message they weren't wanted and didn't show their whiskery heads again.

But as it turned out I didn't see a cockroach of any kind for another year, even in deepest darkest Australia and I only finally caught up with one in the Blue Mountains towards the end of our stay in Oz when I found one preening himself on my toothbrush in the bathroom and, oh boy, did he get it, not with a vacuum cleaner but with a well-aimed crack of a rolled-up copy of the Australian newspaper. Then I fed him to the family lizard which, I guess, has a certain ecological ring about it which even Nathan might have approved of.

3: The Great Journey Goes Nowhere

The adventures and larks our imaginations constructed prior to our taking off on our jaunt around Australia in a camper van were little short of amazing. We were going to take long journeys through the Bush, I thought, making friends with kangaroos, lost in wonder at fiery sunsets and big nights full of stars. We would hunt wild animals with spears and, when hungry, we would roast crocodiles over open fires. Everything – our whole beings – would become rebooted in an adventure like no other.

In reality we had got our Winnebago but had moved barely ten yards in it. After almost two weeks of persistent endeavour, we were still stuck in the same campsite in the pouring rain. My world darkened further when the previous Sunday, Cardiff City Football Club were battered by six goals to two by crummy Liverpool. I ask you. Poxy Liverpool. This Mr Tan has just got to go.

The Winnebago saga had begun three days after we got to Manly when we found the headquarters of the Sydney Recreational Vehicle Group next to a huge camp site crammed with campers and caravans in Narabeen, a small town further along Sydney's Northern Beaches. After a few minutes I decided on a high and handsome second-hand camper which had bed space for five, a bathroom with toilet and shower, solar panels, a microwave and a huge driving area which would suit Liz. The van was not without a few problems which the dealership said it could quickly fix and we agreed to pay A$68,000 for it. The windscreen needed replacing but within a week or so we could be on our way.

The first hurdle we needed to jump was to register the ownership with the road traffic authority. Liz took on this apparently simple task until it came to proving she was who she said she was. Liz is good at amiable negotiation – unlike me who will shout a lot and get abusive when thwarted – but even she couldn't crack the obduracy of this bunch because they wanted to see her Christian name, in full, on some sort of official form or household bill. Her passport wasn't enough, her debit and credit cards weren't enough. There was a lot of e-mailing to Wales for copies of utility bills and Liz trudged back and for to the rego office three times where they kept moving the goalposts about what it was exactly they needed. Finally she took out an Australian bank account – which they could have told her at the beginning, but didn't – so they finally accepted she was who she said she was.

As the end of the next week approached, with further repairs needed, which hadn't been made clear at the time of purchase, we knew we were well and truly stuck on the site and whiled away many hours playing Freecell which is not quite up there with roasting freshly caught crocodile. And if you play it for too long you never get to sleep at night as all those numbers keep rolling through your mind rather like playing an endless and silent game on a cosmic fruit machine.

The most exciting it got was when we found ourselves repelling swarms of ants which kept invading every corner of the van before being doused with a good squirt of insecticide. Another way of keeping them out, a neighbour told us, was to circle our van wheels with talcum powder because ants hate walking over talcum powder and this did turn out to be true.

We scurried back to Manly while the remaining repairs had to be done but, when we returned, they said they still couldn't fix the driving seat and had jammed a few pipes under it to stabilise it. The seat is perfectly OK as long as you don't try to adjust it, they said. This was no use at all and I freaked out. Further calls were made and finally they said they had located a new seat, still in its wrapper, but the warehouse had been flooded in a storm so we should get it soon.

Then we got a taste of Australian weather, which we weren't expecting, and that left us shaking for hours.

There is a dull, lone thwack of a snare drum at the beginning of Bob Dylan's Like a Rolling Stone which, for me, always announces the beginning of the verbal and musical wonders which pour forth.

There was a thwack something like that in the blue sky above our campsite and within five seconds the whole of this blue sky had turned black and there was a crack of thunder and a dazzling flash of lightning. The thunder bellowed again and the rain came pouring down thicker than any rain I had ever seen before, smashing on to the roof of the Winnebago in an unstoppable, unrelenting downpour which seemed to be trying to pull apart every joint in the rig. We couldn't even see out of the windows as lightning flashed again, illuminating yet more rain. We were camped under a huge pine tree when, with another avenging crack of lightning, it looked as if the whole tree had fallen down around us in a tremendous swoosh. There were huge branches lying everywhere and we could see that the main branch had just missed us by inches.

Within minutes this flash storm had stopped and people from neighbouring vans came over to see if we were all right. Well we were, sort of. Had the tree fallen directly on us I'm sure our trip would have been over before it had even begun. But the tree had scared us and, when we told the dealership about our problems and our uncertainty about carrying on with our plan to travel in one of their vehicles around Oz, they produced a bunch of new workmen we didn't even know they had, who fixed the driving seat and a number of other issues and, the next morning, WE WERE ON OUR WAY.

***

We hit the Pacific Highway and immediately became the slowest moving vehicle in New South Wales. Everyone flew past us and, although we did pass two big vehicles going uphill, they immediately struck back and roared past us going down. You could just see the thought patterns of those brawny tattooed truckies, who weren't having any of those camper things overtaking them, particularly when driven by a sheila.

The surrounding countryside was a strange tangled mixture of tropical trees and shrubs and I was intrigued by how the tree trunks all seemed black until it dawned on me they had all been charred by forest fires. The sudden flare-ups of devastating forest fires are an accepted part of life out here. Most are started by lightning strikes and a few are started deliberately but a lot more are started by Forest Rangers to control the forests. They have to be particularly careful with the gum trees which are packed with oil and will burn ferociously.

Our biggest surprise was the state of the roads – all bitumined, clean and straight as broomsticks. You could sit in your rig, tie up the wheel and fall asleep knowing that you would get to wherever you wanted to get to merely by keeping your foot on the accelerator. Our earlier fears of disappearing down potholes or getting stuck in bogs disappeared. These were the most wonderful roads we had ever driven on and what is more, we were told, we could drive on bitumen right around Australia.

Our first stop was a McDonalds which I must admit is always a disappointment to Liz who clearly thinks I should become a bit more of a gourmet in my old age. (This never stops her eating the whole burger and all of the fries, it should, in fairness, be noted.) But McD's burgers are great for travellers; they're cheap and quick and you always know what you are going to get while the fries are the best in the world. The toilets are also always clean too and you can get free wi-fi which, we suspect, they switch off if the place gets too crowded since they don't want to get their tables clogged up with too many dreamers writing novels or travel books on their lap-tops.

My one real problem with McD's though is that many of their clientele are fat and built like dumper trucks. The fat men clearly don't give a damn what they look like with their bellies drooping down below their vests and almost touching their kneecaps. The fat women, on the other hand, all appear to be of a certain age who might have had good figures when they were young but along came a couple of kids and they just let themselves go. Such women not so much walk as waddle along very slowly and it wouldn't all be quite so bad if they didn't wear such tight-fitting trousers and tops which reveal their Michelin man bulges right up the length of their bodies.

What is even more horrifying than all that (and what I might sometimes watch with sly astounded glances) is the way they often take a Big Mac with both hands – two burgers in a thick bun, with slices of processed cheese and slivers of lettuce - and jam it straight into their mouths and hold it there, eyes half-closed with a kind of ecstasy before beginning to clamp their jaws tight and start giving it a good old chew.

I confidently await the day when they will actually bite off their fingers while they are doing this and end up being photographed on the front page of a newspaper coming out of the restaurant without their fingers. DINERS IN FINGER LOSS SHOCK.

On the way back out to the parked Winnie we spotted a stray pair of ragged knickers stuck to our TV aerial on top of our rig. Don't ask how they got there – and on the very first leg of our journey - because I just don't know.

***

We spent our first night on the road on the shores of Lake Macquarie and could have parked right in the middle of the Snowdon aviary in London Zoo. Everywhere there was the sound of birds screeching and fighting: noisy cockatoos, a whole row of fat pelicans sitting in a line on some sort of bench on the lake itself and gangs of quarrelling parrots. A really noisy gang of about ten ducks was busy quacking about in all this.

I sat out on my canvas chair next to the van, intrigued by all this bird activity when a rather portly man wandered past carrying a box of tinnies and parked himself on a bench on the edge of the lake. Interestingly he had the sweetest little bird, a cockatiel, on his shoulder who, it turned out, lived with him. He was a Brummie, perhaps predictably, because they are all silly putty in Birmingham, who had lived here for thirty years and clearly loved his little bird. His biggest worry was that his bird would get snatched by the local eagle which had been keeping a hungry eye on him. That would be a disaster for our Brummie friend who relied on his bird to get him home when he'd emptied too many tinnies. And it wouldn't exactly be the bird's greatest moment either.

I asked him if he should perhaps be more worried by all the pelicans hereabouts?

Oh no. Pelicans don't eat birds.

Well, you're dead wrong there, I said. I knew a pelican called Daphne who lived in St James' Park in London and she was always eating small ducks and upsetting the children. She was finally packed off to Whipsnade Zoo where they had undisclosed ways of dealing with cannibals in their midst.

I'll remember that, he said, but meanwhile don't you go feeding the ducks here. They're feral and not very nice.

This is one bit of advice I should have taken. That evening, as Liz was making dinner, I was standing at the van door when these ducks rolled up in a big gang and I flung them a few slices of brown bread. They all went nuts, grabbing the bread and one another's throats or yelling at me for more.

A little later I wandered off to the campsite's toilet and was sitting there quietly, minding my own business, as you do, when I became aware that the same gang of ducks was outside the door all yelling for some more of that brown bread which could have had drugs in it the way they were all banging on. Well they weren't having any more and I strode back to the Winnebago, locked the door and turned up the television since they had all followed me home and were shrieking outside. I might have become like that Lorenz bloke: I'd just given those ducks a few bits of bread and I'd become imprinted on their brains as if I were their mother.

I didn't think any more of them and slept well through a night of rain. But when I opened the door early the next morning I found the same old gang bathing in the puddles on my new tarpaulin and drinking the water too. This was too much. Get lost, I shouted at them. Go and shower somewhere else.

About half an hour later I was watching the football in the campsite recreation room and the poxed Liverpool, who had recently beaten my team, were beating Southampton through one fluky goal by Stevie Gerrard. I was down in the dumps, which is where I always am when Liverpool score, when the door opened and in crashed that same gang of ducks, surrounding me and shrieking for more brown bread. Maybe it did have drugs in it.

I couldn't take any more of this. We're moving on towards the wine fields of the Hunter Valley where I was already worrying I might get very drunk indeed. Something was already telling me this trip might turn out to be the severest test of my sobriety.

***

It was about now, still early in our journey, that I began developing a major worry about what kind of book I wanted this to be. My first thoughts had been to make it a comedy. A lot of my friends and family often say I should forget about God and stick to comedy. You're funny, they often say. You make us laugh and, if you went down that road you might even make some money. But when I look around at the world I don't see much – no, I don't see anything – to laugh about and I've never written one word for money anyway. If you write for money you soon stop being a real writer.

Also Jesus never saw anything to laugh about: there is no record of him ever smiling or telling a joke. He simply went among the people and told them the truth.

***

Everywhere I turned in Australia I saw disturbingly beautiful scenes and, in those savagely colourful sunsets, when all heaven broke loose in our wondering eyes, I could also clearly hear the breaking heart of God. He was there in the sky in every sunset and I was later to see and hear him just as clearly in the reed-filled billabongs and the emus and kangaroos who kept bouncing along the roads next to us as we drove, all as mad as tennis fans.

So God was sort of in my life again. He always turns up when I wish he wouldn't except there were no major disturbances or searing visions at the minute – as had happened to me in the past – and the best I could do, I guessed, was to listen out for his words or gauge his feelings and, providing they weren't too turbulent, writing about them accordingly. I couldn't make this a simple comic romp around Australia, certainly not with him around. He was too full of heartbreak these days, his eyes too full of tears and my main problem was that he had once told me all about it.

I completely got it and could never turn my back on him even if I wanted to.

In one shattering series of visions fifty years ago he had explained to me why and how terrorists are scorching the world everywhere; why young men were shooting up the schools and campuses, particularly in America, and how the media was managing to spray messages of death all over the world causing murder and strife everywhere those messages landed. He also enabled me to understand how the world has started communicating in the language of explosions and beheadings. We are living in an age of black rain set up by our romantic, violence-loving media, he told me, which is spreading street riots, shootings and terrorism everywhere.

I have written about all these ideas before in my books and can't say that I've got many – if any – followers who believe me.

Yet what I am saying is the truth, I know, so I have to keep grappling with the central revelations of my life if only because I don't have any other options. I keep trudging down a dark and stormy pilgrim path simply because I can't do anything else.

I could never toss my youthful visions aside because I had become fed up with them or they didn't make me any money or I didn't have any followers. I was stuck with them for ever and that's the way it was.

***

But first there are real stories about Australia to be dug out and the glories of reality to tend to. You only ever find real truths in reality, I believe, and that's where the media always gets it so wrong because it always rejects reality in favour of fantasy, murder, riot and lies. But I guess we'll get to that soon enough. Maybe we won't but, knowing him as I do, we probably will. It is a burden I've been chosen to shoulder until I drop.

4: Chinese Superglue and String

I didn't spend long working in the media – about fifteen years – and since then I've written a good few books complaining about it, the latest being A Reporter's Tale. I believe as an article of faith that in its persistent pursuit of violence, cruelty and perversion the media has become a huge agent for lawlessness in the modern world, provoking crime and violence everywhere and then setting up this violence as a fashion with which nitwits need to keep up.

The day the world wakes up to such insights, I believe, will be a great day for the world and a very bad day for our terrorists.

But I am completely in favour of news reporting – especially when it is not lapping up blood and mindless violence – and it often amuses me to find that my old reporting instincts have remained intact over the years. I can always sniff out a good story when I hear one and love to talk to people, as I fish for more evidence to back up the story before presenting my findings in an entertaining and readable way. Even a fair bit of my novels have been largely reportage. That's what I do.

I heard this story on the Arcadia, the P&O ship that brought us to Sydney. We were having breakfast and a strange, diminutive couple came and sat in front of us. They didn't say anything to begin with and, unusually, I left them to it, more interested in the way the husband was peeling a banana. No banana could ever have been peeled like this banana.

He took a good three minutes to get the skin off but even longer taking off the minute veins that ran down the side of the flesh before cutting the lot up into neat chunks to eat. You could also see his utter fastidiousness in the way his clothes had been meticulously ironed. The wife seemed even odder although she did manage to eat her banana without quite so much fuss as her husband.

Finally she said a few words to us and I asked her what she did. Oh, she said, we've done a lot of road travelling over the past ten years and we once wandered around the Bush for three years without going home at all. We're what you call Grey Nomads.

I loved this attractive phrase as soon as I heard it. The Grey Nomads of Oz. Then she said something I found even more compelling. What you've got to remember is always take superglue and a few balls of string with you when you go on the road. You can fix anything with that. But remember the superglue must be Chinese, the husband chimed in, having finally - after about half an hour - finished his banana.

There are thousands of Grey Nomads on Australian roads, she went on. They're all fleeing from something, all looking for a new life.

A lot more was said over that breakfast and what happened then was what always happens when I get a sniff of a good story: I had a strong and continuous twinkling in my nether bits. It's not a sexual thing, just a ripple of strange excitement that starts between the legs and gets straight into the blood. What a story. On the Road with the Grey Nomads of Oz. What were they all doing? What were they escaping from?

After that breakfast I occasionally dropped the words Grey Nomads into my conversations with Aussies returning home on the ship and it usually produced something. There were Grey Nomad camps where they got up late, boozed all afternoon and then, after a good dinner, were all in bed by nine o'clock. They all looked out for one another and often travelled in threes to keep an eye on one another particularly in the rainy seasons. If a young woman was on her own they always insisted on learning where she was going and what time she expected to return before she was allowed to go out.

They were all looking for meaning in the end of their lives. Well, we're all looking for that, and maybe this was a chance for me and Liz to find some for ourselves.

***

This morning we were packing up to leave Lake Macquarie – and I had bunged my ducks a few farewell bits of brown bread – when I struck up a conversation with my neighbour, who gloried in the name of Bruce, and he was telling me about his teeth. The story was averagely interesting – as stories about teeth go – since one of his front teeth had gone crook and he was having it replaced. First they had to build a new post for the new tooth and he was offered a choice of bone for it. He could have bone from his arm, which would need an operation, bone from a cow and, most interestingly, bone from a cadaver although, annoyingly, he didn't seem to know where this cadaver would come from. I would certainly want to know where any new tooth of mine came from especially if it was straight out of the mouth of a dead person. I don't think I would enjoy a meal ever again if I thought I was chewing my food with, say, a tooth taken from a serial killer.

Anyway he had settled for a bit of cow and hoped he had made the right choice. The tooth was going to cost him six thousand dollars and the worst part about it was that he had to keep going home every few months to get the next step done. He'd been on the road for over two years.

Really? What did he do?

He was a Grey Nomad.

Aha. So here it was again. He spoke of the way the old were fleeing the cities and going into the wilds, seeking to enjoy the empty expanses of the red centre. Drugs had taken over the cities and moved into the small towns, he added. Escaping into the Bush just made sense even for people of his age. I suppose it could even be seen as an inversion of the romantic ideals of the hippies when they were young, riding out in their Harleys and smoking dope in the desert while making love next to the cacti.

I couldn't learn enough about all this and even wondered if Liz and I could become Grey Nomads, spending the rest of our lives wandering the trackless deserts of Australia. But she didn't seem all that keen when I mentioned that possibility. Not in the slightest in fact.

But yet again I could actually feel Australia challenging me with new thoughts and ideas. I was already half in love with the country and, as Liz drove on, could even feel a sort of newness spreading through my ramshackle old body. This was going to be my last do or die book and I felt a roaring confidence in it, foreseeing travelling everywhere in this wondrous land and finding new aspects of nomadic radiance at every turn.

Through this country, I was sure, I might even be able to reach out and touch God again. I might be able to find him – or he might even find me - although I couldn't even guess, not even the wildest flights of Celtic fantasy, how exactly that might happen.

We might even end up not going home at all and just keep driving down these lovely bitumen roads forever. I had already met a few Grey Nomads who were doing just that and I knew we would be looked after; that there might even be an angel riding on top of our rig, looking out for us as the immigration people searched for us in the Bush anxious to throw us out as soon as our year-long visas had expired.

But how would they find us? The Bush is a mighty big place; people can - and do - disappear into it forever.

5: Breakfast with Dinosaurs

We are standing ankle-deep in a warm, clear sea in a lagoon which may just have fallen off the end of paradise. The water is fringed by a huge arc of sand and green foliage and a gang of kangaroos emerge from the shrubs and trees at the far end of the beach and stand around looking at the water as if about to swim in it. They are a shapeless bunch who start moving towards us before disappearing back into the Bush.

Their silence and stealth suggest they are a war party trying to sneak up on their enemy. Now they come back out on to the sand and give us another right good looking at. There is no sign of aggression, just that dopey, brown-eyed stare, big floppy ears and strange dislocated jaw which looks as if it has recently been pounded out of kilter in a fight.

The water in front of us is full of small fish sniffing around for something to eat and there is only one man moving in the lagoon itself, a treasure hunter carrying two huge metal detectors which both appear to work underwater. He's found all sorts, he says, and you'd be amazed at how many women lose their wedding rings here. He will track these women down if he can, and return their rings. But watch out for stingrays in this water, he adds. They will usually swim away from you but, if you step on one, you'll know all about it. Oh you'll know all about it all right.

The roos have gone away again but I'm sure they are still watching us. Shadows move around in the bushes which might be anything. They can get nasty, I've heard, particularly if they fear you might be about to kidnap one of their little joeys. And if you do feed them a bit if bread, which they judge not to be enough, they might well attack you for more. Not like those ducks in Macquarie then who just kept squawking at you furiously but didn't actually attack you.

We're staying in Arakoon, near the South West Rocks, in the shadow of an old prison. The only adjective that keeps leaping to mind is gorgeous and, as I sit here in the shadow of a tree, I notice that a kookaburra is perched on a branch above me. He is all gussied up in the splendid finery of an Aztec Sun King on his way to his third wedding. His calls are, just, well, jubilant in their happiness and his head big like his beak.

Later the sun starts going down in its usual storm of red tropical rage and I am sitting here in the roasting twilight aware that another group of eyes are close by, watching my every move. The kangaroos are back and they come out on the sand again clearly more relaxed in the semi-darkness, many of them now grazing on clumps of grass in the sand and leaving huge turds behind them. Oddly enough I am not now finding them slightly scary and this is a big step forward. Perhaps I am already becoming Australianised.

When we first arrived in Australia I wanted to kill everything in sight - or at least run away from them as fast as I could - but now I drop a bit of bread a few feet from me and just stand there waiting for the roos to take it, which they duly do, even if they still keep a wary eye on me.

***

The next morning we move a couple of hundred kilometres up the coast and decide to camp wild in a place which revels in the name of Minnie Waters. Others are already camped in clearings in the scruffy woodland on a cliff-top where you can hear the suck and wash of the waves. Here again there are lots of roos dotted about, grazing on grass unconcernedly, not even bothering to look up at us. We find our own clearing and, after the by now ritual row with Liz about whose turn it was to make the tea, which I lose again, I sit outside the van door and watch two young guys who have set up a tent in the clearing next to us. They don't seem particularly friendly at first and are busy feeding a family of kookaburras with freshly cooked bits of meat.

I had already noted this family of kookaburras had been watching us from a nearby tree almost as soon as we had arrived but when our two neighbours produce the meat the birds find them much more attractive and settle down on another tree to watch the barbecue below them.

The mother and father bird stay in the tree looking over the proceedings while the three youngsters are the first down to get their meat and, when they've had their fill, they return to sit next to their parents on the branch and the mother comes down. When she's had enough she flies back to her family and the father flies down for his helping.

It is all done in such a graceful and orderly way and everyone, including the two guys feeding them, seem to know exactly their role as in a well-rehearsed play.

In a way all this might even be a key to an understanding of modern Australia, I think, where the city slickers and the wild things are coming together to satisfy one another's needs. I will see this happening again and again throughout our travels and I want to be part of it too, even if I can never quite see myself actually going out for a barbecue with a huntsman spider, say, or a big venomous snake. Even in my wildest dreams I don't see that happening. And I just don't care what Nathan has to say about it all.

We start talking to the two guys, Josh and Toto from Sydney, finding them friendly and interested in what I was writing. I always tell people I'm working on a book about Australia and that usually opens them up. I tell Josh and Toto I'd like to write about the way they feed the kookaburras and how it all began and they say oh sure but hang around and you'll see something far more amazing than that: breakfast with goanna lizards, a whole family of them live in the rocks on the shoreline just a few yards away and always come wandering up together past their tent about this time, but only if they feel warm enough. They never leave their little homes in the rocks if they judge the temperature to be too low.

I wasn't at all sure I was looking forward to such an encounter; I'd already met up with one of these monsters in Arakoon and can still remember the shock of it. I was eating a bowl of Weetabix and enjoying the sunshine early one morning when one came wandering past, a big, black monster about five feet long who didn't even seem to notice me as he went by. His tongue kept forking out, presumably trying to sniff out food and, I later learned, there are none better for keeping your garden clean. They eat anything and you couldn't catch one, even in the unlikely event you wanted to, since they always head for the trees if they feel threatened.

What I couldn't quite understand was how something which looked so utterly Satanic - as if it had just wandered in from the set of Alien - was clearly so friendly to us humans. Little kids on the Arakoon site even shooed one away with their feet, as you would a pesky dog, if he got too close while they were eating an ice cream.

Aussies just love telling the tale of how these things will actually run up your back and sit on top of your head claiming sanctuary there if they are scared of something. I never believed this story though and, no matter how many times I was told it as "the balls-out gospel truth," still didn't believe it.

Now even though I was keen to get on more friendly terms with wild things like all other Aussies I was not at all keen on meeting up with this local family of goannas here; a mother and father always followed by a pair of skittish youngsters. They usually forage on the beach first thing, Toto says, eating stuff like crabs before coming up here. They will eat almost anything left out for them – even eggshells – but had somehow made it clear to our new friends they would far prefer to have something like runny yolks inside these shells.

"What they really like, almost more than anything else, is bacon and eggs. Hang around for a while and we could all have breakfast together."

I must admit that my heart jumps a few feet up into my throat at the very thought of sharing bacon and eggs with a family of giant lizards so, rather lamely, I say we're on a tight schedule and simply don't have time to share breakfast with them so we'd better get on our way. I know Liz won't have any problems with such a quick exit either. That's the thing about motor homes: if you are scared of anything - or even don't like someone - you can just jump behind the wheel, switch the engine on and stamp on the accelerator.

Yes, I really do want a relationship with all the wild things of Australia but such a relationship is clearly not going to start any day soon. It was going to take time, perhaps a long, long time.

6: The Prison Warder who fell for her Prisoner

As we drove on I perused my swelling notebook with its record of the people we had met on the road so far. Theirs really were remarkable stories and you just could never tell what they were going to come up with next. The Aussies were a dream to interview: I would sit outside my rig reading a newspaper perhaps and barely had to look up at them and they were up and running, telling their life stories for a good half an hour before stopping to take a breath. You didn't even have to think of any questions and the only real difficulty came when you wanted to shut them up.

Random though they might all be I found these stories were becoming a good record of the fellowship of the road: the way, when you came down to it, everyone had a story they were always ready to tell. And the stories were so vivid I often found I didn't have to take any notes since I had total recall of them later.

One woman, Milly, told me she knew her first marriage was over when her husband tried to shoot her. She was vacuuming the house when he grabbed the vacuum cleaner and threw it out into the front garden. Then he tried to shoot her with his shotgun but, fortunately, he was as drunk as a wheel and missed her by a mile. They said goodbye soon after that and she had found a new man who even as we spoke was cooking dinner in their rig, without any help from her, and to whom she had now been happily married for twelve years. Every day with him was bliss, she said, and she couldn't bear to be parted from him for even an hour.

Then there was Mike Gardiner, a retired policeman, grey of hair and soft of voice, who had once been in a charge of the riot squad in Toxteth, Liverpool, where they had once practically invented urban rioting. He had loved every minute of his work, he said, despite the fact he had been badly beaten up several times. When the riots had first started in Toxteth the police simply didn't know how to deal with them and took a real hammering for about three weeks.

The national television cameras turned up and, pretty soon, there was rioting all over the country which, of course, had nothing to do with television news. A BBC report concluded that the rioting had spread because people had simply rung one another up and told each other what was going on in their street. Nothing at all to do with the constant fast-moving imagery of television news then. Nothing.

The police just didn't know how to deal with it all since it kept getting worse and at one stage they developed a habit - after being confronted by a gang of rioters - of forming a circle with their backs to the rioters, holding up their shields and truncheons in the air and singing songs to one another. I almost corpsed with laughter when Mike told me that. It was so silly it just had to be true.

Mike was called in to train a new squad and they got better at crowd control after that, using their Scouse wit to become more friendly with the rioters and indeed becoming so friendly they even agreed what time they would gather on the streets, where they would march to get the riot going properly and even what time they would all knock off for lunch and when they would return to start rioting again.

Mike just loved everything about Toxteth. He told the story of how one morning he was approached by two black men who wanted him to dispose of a naked body. He was a policeman, he pointed out, and really wasn't in the business of disposing of bodies – naked or otherwise - but they insisted he should at least come inside and see what was what. They duly took him into a flat where indeed the naked body of a black man was laid on a bed. So what happened to his clothes, Mike asked and was told that, according to tribal custom, when anyone died everyone else in the tribe was free to come in and help themselves to his belongings including his clothes. Something to do with going out the same way you went in.

What I did discover during my various conversations with such retired arms of law 'n' order was how differently the police acted in those days; how they used to do stuff which they would never get away with – or even get locked up for - today. One retired Manchester policeman, of the same era as Mike Gardiner, told me that, when his chief constable learned that a certain group were planning to start trouble in his city, he actually arranged to meet them and told them, in the strongest possible language, that he had a very tough force and, if they did take to the streets and start trouble, his men would not be making any arrests and there would be far more serious consequences for them.

There was never any trouble in Manchester at a time when Liverpool was awash with it for week after week. Also when the Manchester police confronted someone who was drunk and stroppy they would drive him out to a nearby moor in the middle of the night, fling him out and tell him to walk home and sober up.

I've always been attracted to the company of those who uphold the law, particularly those in the army or police. They always seem to have a certain clear-headedness and dedication to their work even when things get difficult. They also appear to take a joy in solving the big problems which ordinary life can throw up. But, by the very nature of the job, they can be difficult to get talking to your notebook and have a healthy and understandable suspicion of anyone who might be from the media.

***

No such problems with Ron though, a man who had formerly been the governor of most of the main English prisons and who you really could not shut up. He simply overflowed with stories which were always wonderful although there was one which he told me when we met in Sydney that stuck in my mind on the day he told it to me and has stayed there ever since. Even at the oddest moments I think about it, often in the middle of the night. It is just so sad.

One day Ron discovered that one of his better warders had been engaged in a sexual affair with one of her prisoners. Incriminating letters and cards had been found and other prisoners had confirmed it. She was, as they say, bang to rights, and was duly hauled up before Ron for a carpeting.

"Oh Irene how could you have done this?" Ron asked her. "You've had a wonderful career in the prison service. You've always worked hard and now you've thrown it all away."

"I just couldn't help myself," Irene replied, crying copiously. "I've got so old and fat and ugly he was the only man who would ever put his arms around me."

Ron let her off with a severe caution and her career became stronger after that.

***

Byron Bay is seen by many as the holiday playground of Australia and it has an extremely attractive setting on a wonderful curve of sand and a sea of the deepest and clearest blue.

But the trouble with this place is it is very difficult to say what it is all about because it is about just about everything. Hippies cluster on every corner all looking like the stragglers after Charlie Manson's last stand; kids rampage down every lane chasing balls and the suits from the cities come down from their vast glass mansions on outlying cliffs with their pneumatic lady friends all ready for a night of raising hell with everyone else in one of the many clubs and pubs.

In the sea you can often see porpoises bouncing around on the waves and recently a shark in a neighbouring bay actually tracked a swimmer for ten kilometres or so before attacking him. Yet still people swim here in their hundreds. They just don't seem to care and even those who've had a big chunk bitten out of their sides don't seem remotely interested in taking any sort of revenge on the guilty shark. "They were here long before us," one said, bandaged from head to toe with three fingers missing.

We were lucky enough to get a site in the busy camping park in the very centre of town although here, too, it would be difficult to say who our neighbours were since they were from everywhere with many bringing their own brand of manners in their back packs.

One afternoon I decided to have a shower and went over to the shower block where I duly keyed in the code in the door to get

35

in. I opened the door after a fair bit of pressing the wrong numbers and kept it open as a youth walked in followed by another and five more. Not one of them stopped to keep the door open so I could go in myself – they didn't even acknowledge me with a nod – and when I finally did get inside I found they had taken up all the shower cubicles without leaving one for me.

They were Germans and anyone who has ever had to share a shower block with almost any kind of Europeans will know that they take at least a half an hour to wash and re-wash their bits and that's about how long it took before one of them came out again.

***

But we liked Byron well enough, particularly all the bookshops, the cheapish restaurants and the palmists and tarot card readers. I met a film maker and we spent a couple of hours discussing his new film and how the story is always vital. If your film hasn't got a good story line it can never be a good film, I told him firmly. If any scene doesn't help the story cut it. He seemed surprisingly interested to learn this banal advice so I can't think his films were much good.

***

As I mentioned earlier living in a motor home gives you very easy access to people and I immediately discovered that my neighbour in Byron was a cattle farmer in the Queensland outback, perhaps one of the friendliest and talkative guys I've ever come across. Brett Thomas was his name and, as soon as I told him what I was up to and who I wanted to interview, he brought out a pile of maps, told us where to go to find the Grey Nomads, who I had not, up to this point, been able to track down in any number, what the roads were like and how to deal with the millions of flies who wouldn't actually bite you but were always after your sweat.

But his political ideas: oh dear they seemed even more right wing than Genghis Khan's. He's in favour of capital punishment, of course, and would personally lash any thieves or paedophiles with a chain. He worked in the gold mines up north – always for seven days a week – to save enough money to buy his seventeen thousand acre farm which he travels over by plane, when it chooses to work, getting by just with the help of his son Mitchell.

Gays were nothing but trouble, Brett insisted. They can't have children of their own so now they want to get married AND have children. It's not right. God made Adam and Eve not Adam and Steve. Sometimes he got a few gays in his cattle and that always led to trouble in the herd. Cattle hate gays, he said, and will rape and attack them. It becomes carnage all the way and, if only to keep the peace, he had to get them out of the way when they would be taken away to be shot or have their heads cut off.

I've long been thinking of Brett's ideas and they worry me to death. But his life has been anything but easy and he's survived four years of drought. There are also days when thousands of kangaroos come bouncing in the direction of his farmhouse looking for food and water. When they come you can't see the Bush for them and you can feel the ground shaking. He hates kangaroos but doesn't shoot them, he says, because he might risk a year in prison (although that might be just what he's telling me). The state decrees he has to look after kangaroos even though they're eating him out of house and home. The government does have the occasional cull but such culls seem to make no difference to the numbers which keep going up.

So this man had grown his own opinions outside normal, conventional views, directly out of his land and personal experience, I came to understand. He stood alone in the parched Bush with his fine son, prepared to take on anyone who came his way, particularly those who feel entitled to handouts from the state. He will never give in to anyone. They can all shove it where it fits, he likes to say, all his words spiced with a blizzard of foul language.

Despite his extreme ideas, particularly about the gays, which made me very uncomfortable, I liked him a lot. Brett was a hard-working farmer in an unforgiving land with clear, uncomplicated views rather than, say, the woolly two-legged publicity machines like politicians who will say anything or rework their views to advance their cause.

I began thinking I had come to like all the Australians we had so far met: they were lovely – even chips of right wing granite like Brett had his soft side: if his wife ever needed to go to the toilet in the middle of the night, for example, he would get up and go with her. But you did have to know how to handle Aussies, I was discovering. They regard any sort of light satire as an affront, for example, and would soon start avoiding you if you tried any of that clever stuff. Even the biggest bruisers wanted to be liked and, as soon as they learned you were writing a book about them, practically their first question was always "So what do you think of us so far?"

I was touched by this insecurity and as soon as I became more careful about what I said to them – not trying any daft jokes about Aussies for example – the better I got on with them. Also as soon as they relaxed with you they were relentlessly kind and generous. If anything ever went wrong with your rig, for example, you only had to stand outside it looking a bit puzzled and within a few minutes someone would turn up with a spanner in one hand and a screwdriver in the other. "We all grew up fixing engines," one explained.

Yet I could see I was still having deep trouble working out what Australia was about in general. They love the wild image of the larrikin yet the doors of all the clubs and pubs in Byron are manned by muscular, po-faced bouncers who like everyone to sign in and give their age at the door – even me who was well over 70 – and, unbelievably, my address and postcode. Postcode? I could never remember my postcode and, when it looked as if I wasn't going to be let in without one, I rummaged around in my wallet where I found a Press card with my photograph from the Western Mail, the national newspaper of Wales, all of fifty years ago. This card always got me in everywhere in Australia and I began using it all the time. Anything to do with the Press with a photograph on it always impresses the hell out of them.

"The very strange thing about the Australians is that they always think of themselves as anti-everything," wrote John Hirst in his book The Australians. "Their most revered hero is Ned Kelly and their unofficial anthem celebrates an unemployed vagrant who commits suicide rather than being taken in by the police."

Yet this was the very first nation to make the wearing of seat belts compulsory, even on back seats. They made the wearing of helmets compulsory for all cyclists as well as for motorcyclists. They also pioneered compulsory breath tests for drivers to ensure they were not driving under the influence of too much alcohol or drugs. All larrikins eh?

So as we moved from Byron there was much to think about as I tried to deconstruct the Australian psyche, puzzled not just by their undoubted stuffiness but by their great liberality too especially when you consider the huge welcome Sydney lays on for the gays each year when they go there from all over the world for their splendid Mardi Gras.

Their extremely liberal attitude to drugs also came as a big surprise as I was to discover when we arrived in Nimbin.

7: How God took me Prisoner

I need at this point to explain how and when God first took my mind and body prisoner because it not only explains the source of many of my ideas to date – and indeed what I almost constantly think about - but also, most crucially, a lot more about those which will almost certainly come later in this book.

Somewhere in Byron I had decided I really had to tell my story. There was simply no way of avoiding it since, in a way, this was the only important thing that had ever happened to me.

My first real revelation came in an extremely turbulent week in the Sultan Abdul Hamid College, Alor Star, a small town in North Malaya when I was a 23-year-old English teacher there in 1964 with Voluntary Service Overseas.

During my free time in the evening – of which there was a lot – I was writing my first novel which, in all its sick obsessions and preoccupations pretty much reflected the popular culture of our time. My pages were suffused with arcane sexuality and lots of violence, all influenced by my favourite authors at the time: Norman Mailer, Henry Miller, J P Donleavy and James Baldwin.

Colin Wilson, indeed, introduced me to the great and dangerous world of literature and a variety of other authors in his

Outsider. Perhaps he more than any other author made me what I was then.

I also enjoyed any films that featured alienation and freewheeling sex. The red blood of Howl ran through my every vein even if I was never that sure what I was supposed to be revolting against. My novel had become seriously large as it emerged from my chattering Olivetti in the evenings. In my immature ignorance I believed I was breaking new ground with it and was going to change the world.

I had been teaching T S Eliot at the time and found myself increasingly drawn to the old Anglican scholar with the clear depth of his learning, the accuracy of his language and his talent for destructive definition. Yet he was, I could see, almost exactly opposite to the kind of writer I was becoming: T S so balanced and in control and me furious and wild with words and ideas blasting off everywhere hoping they would land somewhere. There was no discipline anywhere in my words as my old philosophy professor had constantly reminded me. Get your language under control, always explain what you mean and you might even make a decent writer, he would say.

My old prof, who believed that everything began and ended with Plato, had the strangest view of me and my abilities, once saying that I was a queer cove, a bit like Rousseau with ideas spewing out everywhere. Yet he was certainly right about my need for discipline although, as it turned out, I didn't get that from my philosophy studies but from my years as a journalist, particularly on the Western Mail, when all my effusions or jokes were hammered out of my words since they always had to be clear, precise and easily understood.

If you read the poetry of Dylan Thomas you will often read words which have no discernible meaning although, if he'd had some of my editors from the Western Mail, whose pencils were famous for their brutality, he would not only have probably ruined all his verbal wordplay but become dull and lost everything that had made him great in the first place. But at least you would have understood what he is saying.

Everyone who knew me had known that I had wanted to be a writer ever since the age of six. It was such a wonderful ambition I thought and always impressed the hell out of impressionable young girls. If I hadn't become a writer, I thought I might have become a rock 'n' roll star. That would have been alright.

***

As we were ploughing on through The Wasteland in Alor Star I asked my sixth formers at the college – a formidably bright bunch who wanted to learn everything – to write me an essay on romanticism and was surprised at what came back. "A romantic is one who goes in persistent search of the violent, the perverted, the melancholy and the cruel," one had written. "The romantic always revels in sexual inconstancy," said another. "The romantic often cannot tell the difference between dreams and reality," was another disturbing line for me. "The romantic is always drawn to the supernatural, the weird and the exotic. His natural medium is despair."

Well that settled that. T S was a classicist and I a romantic. Almost all of my pupils' essays before me had unerringly described the contents of the novel I was writing even though none of my essayists had read one word of it. I felt like a crook who had been comprehensively exposed.

It was a Friday afternoon with a free weekend beckoning and, if only to use my characters to give me some company, I was settling down to a few days of quiet composition in my room in

43

the college hostel. Apart from a mynah bird, which one of my pupils had brought me, I was certainly lonely in that period and perhaps what was to happen to me might have been very different if, say, I'd had a girlfriend there. But there were simply none around in Alor Star or, more accurately, none whose families would allow their daughters to go out with a white foreigner.

It was another hot night and geckos were running around the ceiling chasing flies. My mynah bird was sitting on its perch near my typewriter and a blue film had formed over his eyes. His body was listing slightly and wings shivering. Just when he looked as if he was going to topple off his perch, his claws grasped it again and he righted himself, his eyes jerking open to reveal the extent of that sinister blue film. I offered him a grasshopper but he jerked his beak away snootily only to begin listing again. If only you knew the trouble I had getting these grasshoppers in the first place. Then those glazed blue eyes of death opened wide and his body plummeted forwards, landing with a loud thud on the floor. His legs were pointing up into the air and his claws clenched.

The thud made my heart jump and a wave of grief broke over me as I went down on one knee before him. The breeze from my fan was rustling his feathers and I was sure I could hear the pattering of the geckos' feet. One lost his footing and slipped down the wall before dashing back up again. Mere gravity didn't seem to have any effect on those things. The moths fluttering around the light sounded like hurrying bats.

I lit a cigarette and attempted to blow smoke rings but the fan dissipated them before they formed. I was stretched to breaking point and very scared. A rustling sound in the typescript of my novel made me jump sideways and I knocked over a chair with a resounding crack. Something was about to happen, that was for sure. My mind slipped and shifted as if about to shatter into smithereens. High walls were hemming me in and I could not see how I was going to scale them.

I sat on my bed feeling tired when a huge luminous fungal growth began rising up out of my manuscript. I lit another cigarette and sighed as the ball kept swelling. It glowed ferociously and brightly coloured veins wormed their way through it. Sometimes an idea would shoot to the surface before diving back into the heart of it, causing the whole fungus to shiver. Faces moved around its translucent interior: smiling faces, mocking faces, strange faces.

I took a long drag on my cigarette and exhaled slowly. By now my hands were shaking so badly I could barely get the cigarette into my mouth. I had understood immediately what this fungus stood for – the poisoned and poisonous growth of my own romanticism. Even in my trembling shock I saw how faithfully this fungus represented all the rotten emblems of my mind. How it displayed the way my thoughts had become corrupted by violence, cruelty and perversion. This poison had been introduced into my system by books, films and plays. All these had shaped me – the opium fantasies of Thomas de Quincey, the sexist brothel ravings of Henry Miller, the obsession with violence of Norman Mailer; the brooding melancholy and despair of Ingmar Bergman, the crime worship of Colin Wilson and the rebellion of John Osborne. All there.

I tried to stand up but my body wouldn't let me. I couldn't smoke because my shaking hands had frozen. I was clothed but suddenly felt naked. Then, as slowly as it had grown, the fungus began shrinking and my body was released. I thought it was all over.

But I was wrong. I sat up and looked into the mirror feeling I had smashed my face into it with different parts of my face reflected in the different shards of broken glass.

45

When I finally stood up something hot and quick darted right down inside me and I went spinning around in a world in which nothing at all made any sense.

The ideas of my manuscript were sweeping through my mind like swarms of angry bees. I was staring down a well with a cyclone blowing up out of it and I had to hold the top of my head tightly with both my hands for fear the roof of my skull would blow off. Ideas were leaking out everywhere, through my fingers, eyes and ears. I kept trying to punch my disintegrating skull back into place but struck only sparkling jumbles of nonsensical ideas.

I finally managed to escape my room and, with my hands on my head, like a prisoner of war, walked into the town. For the following few days I was seldom aware of myself as an individual as I stumbled on through those uncaring streets, getting lost and seeing fearful visions. Occasionally one of my pupils, seeing I was in a real mess as I stared up at the empty night, would take me back to my room.

One night I had a vision of the world. I saw a silvery plain with matchstick people milling about on it. Tiny ideas were flitting between their heads in looping arcs and lightning dashes. A cliff towered over the plain and, all along the cliff edge dark and demonic bands of artists and communicators – the whole of our media indeed - were loosing off wild volleys on to the people below who were all jumping on each other's backs and fighting savagely. I understood then that the world was but a jungle of ideas in which the artists and communicators of the world – the romantic artists of the world, who were all drawn to its savagery and violence - were actually corrupting the people on the plain.

But there was a bigger story here for me in particular: the whole world was being attacked by people like me since, with my novel, I had been seeking to join in the attack as well. I was one of them!

***

My pupils again found me out in the paddy fields staring upwards at the sky. When they took me back to my room it was a complete mess with papers scattered everywhere and my dead mynah bird still lying on the floor in the middle of it all.

But in all this chaos there was one thing I knew almost as a fact: I had not so much been ejected from the romantic fog as hurled out on my ear by a mighty force. God alone knew what had happened to me and, in this case, that seemed perfectly apt because I was pretty sure that God had done it in the first place. He had decided that he didn't want me to carry on like this any longer and had bashed me up good. Where once I was a cocky young punk whose books were going to change the world I was now a broken man whose books and ideas would never be believed by anyone. Even as the visions were firing up and my brain felt it was going to literally explode, I knew I was going to be saddled with them for ever and would never be able to lay them down.

And that's pretty much how it worked out particularly after I escaped from Alor Star to Penang and way above this teeming city I saw a vision of black rain which opened up in the clear blue sky, with small drops at first and a long shiver of darkness which actually, for a moment, divided that sky. Then there was a collection of small brown wheels which were moving around together slowly like the internal components of an old steam engine. The wheels speeded up and black drops began falling out of them, slowly at first and then hurriedly. It turned into a complete downpour and, as quickly as it had come, it all disappeared and the sky was a clear blue again. It may have lasted for ten seconds but, put another way, it has lasted for ever in my mind and indeed became the mainspring for my twenty or so books. I still can't look up at any blue sky anywhere without half-expecting to see that vision of black rain again.

The real problem with these visions – and why I could never cast them aside - was that I have always believed in their complete integrity and insight, always saw them as an accurate, if brief, picture of a world in violent change and *why it was happening*. Mainly I believe they reflected God's despair at what was happening to his world.

***

So when the Hungerford massacre took place on August 19, 1987, in which Michael Ryan shot and killed fifteen people, including his mother, I understood immediately that Ryan had been working under the influence of the murderous black rain of the violent and romantic Rambo film narrative which had captured his imagination. We can work out that easily from the way Ryan wore the same clothing (including bandana) as Rambo; he also employed the same forest survival techniques and both had similar carbines wearing similar bandoliers of ammunition on their shoulders. Both felt rejected; both felt the world had given them a bad deal.

I wrote extensively about this massacre in the Sunday Telegraph, The Man who Thought he was Rambo, which was well-received almost everywhere but predictably dismissed by Sylvester Stallone who went on to make many more such films. He admitted he could never sue me because Rambo was a fictional character.

There is also a clear reason why our riots continually spread through the world, I believe, not because people everywhere are suddenly feeling a sense of injustice but because they have all been watching the fast-moving, deeply influential imagery of television news. The riots in Toxteth and Tottenham were all followed by rioting throughout England. This is the way the black rain now works in our world even if our broadcasters persistently deny they have such influence. Bright and clever and articulate as so many of them are they just do not understand what they are doing.

In recent years we have seen how the Arab spring also grew out of the fast-moving violent imagery of television news, destabilising governments in the Middle East which almost all collapsed overnight. Indeed if you want to know why people are fleeing the instability of such countries as Libya, with many drowning in the Mediterranean - as I write - you could no worse than look at the way those governments were destabilised by the black rain of television news. Many blame other factors, of course, but it's only ever the imagery of television news. You never have to look any further. If all those governments had managed to switch off television news from such as al Jazeera they would all be going quite well still. Romantics all love the falls of government but such events always have hopeless and even murderous consequences for those caught up in them.

Only yesterday, back home here in Wales I sat and cried as I watched on television news the army thugs gassing and clubbing those poor migrants, together with their women and children, as they tried to cross the Macedonian border. I have to grant that those television pictures did a good job in telling us what was happening to those migrants but few will probably understand that it was those selfsame cameras who set off those migrant problems in the first place, causing instability and anarchy everywhere throughout the Middle East until the migrants had been forced to leave their homes, reviled by everyone, greeted by abuse and even murder as they are pursued by war and rumours of war.

So one way or another I still had a lot to worry about as we trundled through the Bush in our Winnebago with the black rain pouring down on almost every corner of the world and, as I was to discover later, particularly heavily here in Australia.

Yet what most saddened me was that my ideas still seemed to have no real credibility, particularly in the minds of other people. My ideas were often dismissed as merely my opinions and therefore worthless. That was indeed why an entry about me was turned down by Wikipedia; one of the editors there deemed that what I had written in my books were merely my own views and there was therefore no point in taking them seriously.

This life as a freelance prophet is no good at all. The people killed all the prophets that God sent to Jerusalem and, to be perfectly honest, I really should have become an estate agent. I have always written great ads for all the houses I have sold and made pots of money too. But I guess I'm stuck with this career as a freelance prophet since I've found myself unable to do anything else. And, of course, as I have said often enough before, I believe in the integrity and insight of my visions absolutely. There is always that.

For someone who has found himself so far out on his own I have no doubt at all that what I am saying is true and that, when the time is right, which might even be after my death, God will raise up my work and show it to the world. But when? That's another thing about God I know for sure; he only ever works in his own time, way and pace. Nothing and no one ever hurries him.

8: "A Dingo has stolen my margarine"

It is my 73rd birthday and I'm thinking some kind of celebration is in order as we drove through the blazing Aussie sunshine of northern New South Wales and into a town called Nimbin. From the high winding roads leading into Nimbin we could spot communes dotted around in the woodlands and there were high cliffs which didn't seem attached to any mountain ranges. In the streets they do stuff like bong throwing, rolling giant joints or campaigning for whatever hippies might be campaigning for that week.

Liz and I are sitting in the main street discussing how my birthday bash might go. This street is like nothing you have ever seen: a cross between a strange Disney theme park and a few scenes out of The Wire, the television cult hit about young druggies in Baltimore. Names of the garishly coloured shops give a few more clues as to how Nimbin keeps going with no visible means of support: Tribal Magic, Happy High Herbs, Perception, Nimbin Hemp Embassy.

Lots of weekend freaks drift past, all dressed in Sixties gear. There are kaftans and dirty bare feet, headbands and the wild-eyed looks of those who recently got really high and are not about to come down again before next Christmas. The fish and chip shop is called Stoned Fish. You can see that when this lot die they all want to be cremated and have their ashes scattered over the Sixties.

That's the real problem with hippies: they seem unable to grow up, it's always the Sixties with them.

This is a good place to have a birthday although I'm still not sure what form it might take. The trouble is I no longer drink alcohol, but I do have a few early ideas. NO DEALING has been painted on the side of one of the post boxes. But where do you get the dope and what's all this drug paraphernalia doing in the head shops? What are they for? One shop is advertising Brain Dead Liver Tonic but I can't see my birthday party swinging along on that.

We drive down a short hill and find the public camp site which has a good shop and an excellent swimming pool. There was a bunch of koalas living in the high eucalyptus tree behind where we are camped, we were told. My immediate neighbour is an elderly man called Geoff and I discovered he too is a Grey Nomad and I wanted to hear his story. He had sold his house eight years ago, he said, and was now suffering from a number of complaints including arthritis, depression and anxiety. He didn't think he was going to last long but certainly didn't want to die in his old house where the neighbours might not find him for weeks. He was now on the road for as long as he lasted.

So what was he doing in Nimbin? Why here? Aha, here he could get all the cannabis he needed to alleviate his arthritis and he had to have a stiff joint first thing in the morning, as soon as he woke up, to get his hands and body working properly.

A young couple parked next door again, Mathew and Lauren, also knew their time was up when the doctors found they both had massive growths. They took their children out of school and Lauren began educating them on the road until such time as they couldn't carry on any longer. They were occasionally telephoned by the education department to see if the kids were progressing satisfactorily but the department had never posed any problems. Matthew and Lauren also saw themselves as Grey Nomads who would keep travelling until they could travel no more.

I must say I had imagined the story of the Grey Nomads of Oz to be rather more inspiring and colourful than these. I saw them all as cheerfully following the sun around the land - which is why they are often called the Swallows – but the very thought that the first three I'd meet had serious illnesses and were seeing the remainder of their lives out on the road just didn't fit my vision of it. But that was life, I guessed. There's often little inspiring and colourful about real life, particularly when you are in constant pain and coming to the end.

**

We walked back up into Nimbin and wandered around inside the Hemp Embassy which had a dazzling display of everything you could possibly need to get high. There were hemp bags and hemp hats, bags of hemp fertiliser and even hemp coffins in which presumably you could look forward to a long stoned sleep. There were also mountains of literature about sustainability, the environment and woodland, all the issues close to the caring alternative heart including a recent campaign against drilling for gas. There was everything here, in fact, except the drugs and, thinking they might even be the key to a good birthday bash, I approached another customer standing near the bong locker and looking pretty cool. "So where are the drugs then?" I asked him.

"Now then," he said. "You just go over the road and straight down an alley way. Walk down there slowly and just look at them in the eyes. Give them the right look and you'll get snowed under with offers of the stuff."

Liz and I crossed over the road and it really was The Wire on a busy afternoon as we kept looking around at the masses of people and trying to get the right look back. One old crone offered me hemp cake but I turned it down. I really should have taken it, in the light of the subsequent disaster trying to roll my own.

At the end of the alley there were several tables and a large guy doing a deal with a very young black kid busy counting out handfuls of fifty dollar notes. He could have been paying several thousand dollars for about six plastic bags full of dope whose flowering tops had been dried out into small balls the size and shape of Brussels sprouts. The dealer looked at me as he weighed out his plastic bags on tiny scales and asked me what I wanted.

"Well," I said, launching into my imitation of a hesitant Pom who really doesn't know what he wants. "It's my birthday and I don't drink any more so could I have just enough for a couple of birthday joints? Twenty, thirty dollars?"

"You betcha," he said with a conviviality which I'm pretty sure the dealers in The Wire never showed. "But don't go rolling it with tobacco because that's very bad for you."

So I scored in Nimbin, the drug capital of Australia, and Liz and I quickly withdrew from the alleyway looking forward to whatever. I'd known such dope in the Seventies particularly when I was on The Sunday Times where many of them working as journalists there – particularly those we called the Aussie mafia - were at it, often before they started writing.

My real problem was that I hadn't taken a sniff of the stuff for a good thirty years and I'd quite forgotten how it's done.

***

Later it was dark and we rolled out the drugs in the Winnebago. The huge sky above was littered with the most amazing stars and I was sort of hoping that we could get high and wander out into the night and meet up with our new neighbours, the koalas perhaps, who, we've been told, like to come out for a walk in the park at night. Maybe we could all have a good stoned chat.

But I really couldn't remember what to do so Liz suggested we chop up the flowering tops and I rolled it into an extremely bad and floppy joint. Next I got out a new lighter which refused to light and was forced to light the spliff with a taper from the stove. Everything was going wrong. Next thing the whole joint fell apart in my hands with papers and smoking bits of dope scattered all over the floor of the rig.

I sat down defeated, and, a bit late in the day to be sure, Liz commented we should have bought a bong. This was no way to celebrate a birthday. We considered going back into the town and have a few beers or something.

"Well happy birthday anyway," Liz said. "And to be honest I think this is going to be about as good as it gets."

And it was.

***

We finally broke out of New South Wales and drove into the endless farmlands of Queensland. The sheer size and spread of the countryside was almost unbelievable: huge parallelograms of crops spreading to the horizons and disappearing into the skies: no houses or even people but clumps of tropical foliage here and there where you might see huge gangs of white cockatoos screeching at one another as they roosted in the evenings. I did see our first koala here but alas it was lying on the side of the road, flat on its back with claws sticking up, stone dead.

When we did come to small towns they were usually haphazard affairs of clapboard houses and small shops, all flung down around the main street like those in old Wild West films. You half-expected to come across tumbleweed and gunslingers. Certainly their street and place names seemed to be culled from such films: Dead Man's Gulch, Possum Creek, Hang Man's Cliff. Tomorrow we are hoping to be camping in Dogwood Creek.

Occasionally there was a twisted corrugated church sitting there, patiently waiting for a merciful hurricane to put it out of its misery. God is not doing too well in such places, you sense.

There are other foreign influences in this country. Many of the names are English, Scottish or Welsh. There is Cardiff, Aberdare, Llangothlin (their spelling) and a Swansea which is little more than a short row of shops. There's also the lovely Newcastle with a whole range of modern shops and galleries and I often picture the early settlers here; homesick Poms who would sit around a table, poring over a map of Britain and naming the places here after themselves or their long lost hometowns.

***

Last night we camped on a site in Toowoomba and while Liz prepared dinner I sat on my chair outside chatting to those passing us, usually en route to the toilet or for a shower or struggling to carry their waste to the appropriate hole, many of them brimming over with wee. The Walk of Shame, they call it.

Only this morning a neighbour told me about her last site where there were lots of dingoes foraging around the vans. One woman came back to find a dingo inside her van and it instantly ran off with a tub of margarine in its mouth. Margarine! A nice steak or even a fat baby I could have understood. But not a tub of margarine.

The next man to stop in front of me was in good form, doing a wonderful imitation of Edna Everage as he told me about how some Aussies like to dump their rubbish like old push bikes on their roofs; what kind of fish he likes and how to catch them. But then he dropped a smelly stone directly into the pool of our conversation.

"It is simply not possible to like Aborigines. They draw their social payments and just drink it all away. They mess up the houses we have given them and never repair anything. They never pay a bill and, when they're broke after a few days of drinking, they're back down the social saying they're starving. All they ever do is take the piss."

He went on like this and I wasn't too taken back by all his vitriol because I had already heard four or five such anti-Aborigine rants. On the ship sailing over here I had mentioned, as a bit of a joke over a dinner, I was planning to buy a big camper in Sydney then take a few Aborigines with us who would dash off paintings as we travelled through the land which we would then sell from town to town as we do in our own art gallery back home in North Wales. All my Aboriginal painters would be paid well; there was no question of them being exploited.

I might as well have said I was planning to shoot every Aborigine I came across. There was uproar everywhere I told this story. The best I can ever do with Aborigines, the consensus seemed to be, is to ignore them all and never even speak to them. Don't even set up eye contact. We've tried everything but it was all a waste of time, they said.

Maybe the situation really is as difficult as everyone keeps saying it is. I just don't know but I am hoping I will find an Aborigine who can tell me their side of the story.

But I wasn't holding my breath and we could see that their alienation went far deeper than perhaps anyone had yet imagined when we learned that, back in the Fifties, Aborigines were officially classified as animals under the Flora and Fauna Act of Australia.

***

I was well aware that drink can bring with it huge problems and it had certainly done so for me when I was a lot younger. I was secretly pleased with myself that I had so far resisted the call to drink and drugs this trip. We had somehow not gone ahead with the planned dope party and I managed to stay away from the Nimbin bars, just settling for a walk instead, up and down the main street where the druggies had all come out in the warm night to take the air and a right mess most of them looked.

Liz and I had decided – although it wasn't anything like a formal agreement – that we wouldn't drink alcohol at all on this trip. Liz liked to give it a go now and then but our thinking was that we didn't want to get up every morning and drive up those long roads with anything like a hangover, particularly with mad kangaroos and emus wandering around.

We needed to have clear minds which would give us the edge in what might become a difficult journey and, of course, we would save a huge amount of money which would otherwise be spent on drink.

I could never drink small amounts anyway: I was a lifelong alcoholic who, if he drank one, always wanted a hundred. That's the way drink always worked for me and, why, so often it had got me into trouble, particularly when I was a journalist in the early days of my marriage. For me drink had always opened doors which should have stayed well and truly closed. Yes, it was either all or nothing for me when it came to drink and, just for now, it was nothing.

There was also the question of my health, which had never been brilliant particularly in my drinking days. Yet here I was embarking on my seventies, unlike my old colleagues on the Sunday Telegraph, say, who had all pretty much drank themselves to an early death. (There's not one left from the features room when I was there.) At our age life is pretty much a matter of giving our bodies the best chances we can, I think. As we get to the end of things it's all we've got to get us through and the really interesting thing about drink is that, like drugs, they are both poisons that make you feel better while killing you at the same time.

Such thoughts had been provoked by our walk around the druggies of Nimbin late on our last night there and seeing they were clearly all going to be lowered into their hemp coffins even earlier than all those journalists I had once worked with.

One young girl in particular had caught my eye in the street: a blonde with a truly sensational face, a big Roman nose and high cheekbones, who was clearly zonked out of her brain. She had one of those stoned smiles beloved of druggies when they think of something smart but won't let on what it is and was rummaging in her handbag for something she couldn't find. It wasn't cannabis that had got her into that state but something far heavier like heroin, I guessed, and, just watching her, I knew she too would soon be getting one of those hemp coffins. The only thing she could really look forward to was dying happy.

As we drove on I kept thinking of that zonked blonde sitting in the street waiting to die just as, rather strangely perhaps, I often thought of the face of that "fat and ugly" warder who had an affair with one of her prisoners, even though I had never seen her face. We collect the faces of such people in our memories and, at odd times, they come back to haunt us. The other night both of them turned up in my mind hand in hand and looking down on me with deep concern as I slept.

9: Exit the town Parade pursued by half a Million Flies

We hit the Warrego Highway – also known as the Road to the Bush – after breaking camp in Dogwood Creek and you could immediately spot the emblems of a harsh and even dangerous countryside we were about to cross.

There were road signs warning of possible floods and others telling of the current risks of forest fires. The land was no longer cultivated and there were frequent huge cactus plants – some a good ten feet high – lining the road like spiky guardians of this barren territory.

We planned to stay in Roma, a township of 6,500 who were celebrating Easter this weekend which would give us a chance to explore the place which had once managed to make huge piles of money out of oil and gas. This Easter celebration of the countryside had attracted a further three thousand visitors, meaning all the hotels and regular campsites were fully booked so we ended up outside the town, under a bottle tree in the car park of the local Gun Club.

As it turned out this was a bit of a mistake since it was a Thursday night, a time when all the members gathered and blasted away at a luckless cardboard target. This constant shooting went on for an almost unendurable three hours. For ten dollars a go, visitors were also given the opportunity to shoot at the target. Not for me though. Even in my sobriety I'm still so shaky I couldn't have hit the fields all around let alone the target itself.

But it was too late to move anywhere and I was already enjoying the other waifs and strays who were moving around the country with us and had ended up here in the Gun Club. This included one who happened to shower next to me, both here and back in Nimbin. He was a drug dealer but there was nothing discreet or slight about him. Indeed he was so large he might have eaten a McDonald's burger twice a day all his life.

I was too scared of him to ask him anything, particularly about his drug dealing, although, in the shower, he liked to sing sweet and plaintive songs about the state of his Irish soul. Unfortunately, the flow of the song was often interrupted as he began coughing his guts up. He smoked his own wares regularly, I guessed.

***

The star event of the weekend came early the following morning with a street parade in which most of the town had clearly joined in. There might have been five hundred taking part in this parade – plus about half a million early rising flies excitedly gathering around the many piles of steaming crap left by the horses. The crowds seemed to enjoy the parade mightily, with many of those on the floats throwing sweets and other goodies at them as they massed on the pavements. I got a free pen courtesy of THE INJUNE DAILY EXPRESS which was really nice and actually worked.

There was certainly plenty of enthusiasm propelling this parade and my heart lifted a few points when a gang of Hells'Angels roared down the main street, except that the lead motorbike had broken down and was being towed by a youth on a scooter. Three of the many vintage cars had also broken down and, as if the whole crocodile was not moving fast enough, along came three of those endless road trains, all impeccably burnished for their great day, but who slowed everything down to the speed of a milk float on the point of breaking down.

I have never seen so many floats with so little floating on them except bunches of excited kids. Of about thirty floats there wasn't one display which had taken more than five minutes to build and there was one with a band on it where the drummer was clearly playing a different tune to everyone else.

Not a new chapter in the history of parades then, although it gave us a good opportunity to watch a town enjoying itself and surrendering to their evident pride in their community. But everything changed that night at the Bull Ride. About six hundred gathered in the local park around a heavily barred ring of sand when, as the time approached, some fifteen cowboys in full regalia lined up to be introduced to the crowd. These cowboys all looked as cool as lollipops with that fixed look of determination which they were all going to employ to subdue the mad bulls who were penned around the back of the ring already snorting with snot and their own determination to shoot the cowboys off their backs as quickly as possible. You need to stay on for a minimum of eight seconds.

What happened was that everyone gathered around the pen, a gate clanged open and all hell broke loose as the bull careered across the ring, spinning around and around or bucking up and down trying to unseat the cowboy hanging on for dear life. If the bull did manage to unseat the cowboy he then, somewhat ungraciously, tried his best to gore the fallen cowboy as other men tried to distract the bull, one by kicking sand into his eyes. Only one cowboy managed to stay on for more than the required eight seconds.

It was one of the vilest events I have ever seen and my sympathies were firmly with the bull. What made everything worse was that an overweight kid, no more than the age of four, on the bench behind me, kept kicking me in the backside with the tips of his crocodile cowboy boots. I kept glaring at him but he was far too preoccupied with a bucket of candy floss and a giant foot-long sausage which had been deep-fried in batter with tomato sauce all over it. These feasts on sticks were called Dagwood Dogs and its red sauce was splattered all over his greedy fat chops.

The rest of the kids there – and there were an awful lot of them, all fat with their fat mothers – seemed to be enjoying themselves hugely while at the same time eating something disgusting. Mums even held up tiny babies to give them a good look at any possible goring. Suitably enough ACDC were blasting out their big hit Highway to Hell on the public address system. Yes, for once, the right music indeed.

***

We finished our four-day Easter festivities in Roma with a wife-carrying contest on the racecourse, an event which plumbed completely new depths in inanity. Hundreds of punters had turned up but there were only two couples on the starting line, one member of which looked suspiciously like the contestant's daughter.

The idea was that husband carried wife around the course while the wife clung on as best she could. Upside down seemed to be favourite, arms around the man's waist with her two legs going backwards over his shoulders. And they're off! One had taken a clear lead when he hit the water jump and the clumsy oaf dropped his poor wife headfirst into the water. The other couple saw their opportunity and the husband actually managed to leap the water jump and make a frenzied dash for the winning post only to fall over in all the excitement a few yards before he got there.

The first prize for the winner was your wife's weight in beer but that was held over for another day because no one had won or even reached the finishing line. I would have thought the wife who nearly drowned in the water jump would have at least qualified for a few pints. But she got nothing either.

***

The great bonus of driving through the Bush is that, far from being monotonous, there is always something new to look at. Whenever you crested a hill on the road there was always an interesting panorama. Here you can look at blackened tree trunks for hundreds, if not thousands, of miles. Those fires seemed to have got almost everywhere with no way of stopping them or even slowing them down.

Then, every fifty yards or so, there was the smashed-up body of a kangaroo with a rib cage picked clean by the marauding eagles and crows who clearly love the easy life of living on road kill. They don't even have to go to the trouble of tracking anything down. The eagles fly away as you approach but, if you run over anything vaguely edible, they are back feeding on the carcass almost the second you have passed.

In other parts whole clusters of trees have been flattened and were lying quite dead and in the same direction suggesting they had all been flattened by the same tornado. The creeks were dried up too and you kept crossing bridges where nothing by way of water flowed underneath, not even a few dribbles. A fat yellow locust, evidently having lost the mother swarm, bounced off our windscreen.

The bitumen roads were still good, wide and straight with those huge road trains bearing down on you now and then, often putting the wind up Liz who still does all the driving and is determined to drive every mile of our journey. Just get out of the way of those road trains, we have been told repeatedly, but there is often no room to get out of their way without rolling down some high camber so we tend to stop and close our eyes, praying not to be knocked into some ditch. I do have a two-way radio for talking to such drivers and reasoning with them to let us through with plenty of spare room. But I haven't a clue how to use it.

Yet we do still keep seeing beautiful things. Most of the trees out this way are a straight green but this morning we spotted a bougainvillea in brilliant and even raucous purple, all its flowers covered in a shimmering quilt of large white butterflies.

***

We had driven two hundred kilometres that morning on the way to the small township of Tambo and, as we approached it, set in a woodland, I remembered another morning, fine like this, when I was in Israel, sweating like this, and following the road to Jericho. That desert was nothing but sand and rock but we took a bend and right there, in the middle of sandy deadness were the palms and banana trees of Jericho. This holy town had been built on the confluence of several rivers, which was why it was alone prospering out here in the desert. The land of milk and honey indeed.

***

That memory firmly locked in my mind as we approached Tambo which had huge bottle trees standing guard on many corners and a fine library and information centre where the acting librarian, another Bruce, told us how he was planning to sell his house, buy a new rig and become a Grey Nomad himself. His health wasn't too good and he wanted to be surrounded by beauty when he died and not lying, whisky in hand, in front of a television with the curtains drawn.

Bruce directed us to the best – and only - campsite around and, as we drove into it, we had to stop because a three-foot long lizard had walked out into the approach road in front of us. This lizard showed an awesome lack of concern about the possibility of being pancaked like all those kangaroos out on the road and indeed just wandered serenely in front of our motionless tyres like some old lady on a zebra crossing knowing that all the rights of way were firmly on her side and she would take as long as she wanted.

So we just there patiently until he got safely to the other side.

10: Elvis has returned to the building

We left Tambo and hit the road to Longreach, the so-called capital of the Australian Outback. The land immediately became harsher and wilder and those kangaroos that weren't mashed up on the road began racing us. More stray emus appeared although they seemed more dainty and diffident than the nutty roos, slipping away into the Bush where, motionless, they often looked like a lot of the other small trees dotted about. More wedge-tailed eagles circled the skies above us still on the lookout for anything we might hit for them. Even this early in the morning we knew we were in for another fly-blown roasting.

One feature I immediately noticed out here was that the food in the roadhouses had become disgusting and, apart from what Liz served up in the van, I can't remember the last meal I had enjoyed. I guess the problem was that most of these roadhouses had no competition and were so far away from any fresh food sources they believed they could serve up whatever swill they liked to fill a hungry passing trade.

Back in Manly and Sydney we'd loved almost every dish we'd had in the restaurants, the plentiful seafood in particular. That was still on offer in many of the roadhouses out here except they deep-fried everything to the extent everything looked and tasted pretty much the same. Deep frying everything disguised the fact that it all came out of the freezer where it may have lain for years, I guessed.

Somewhere under it all you might find a small pile of badly cooked chips. I stared hard at one dish in front of me, half expecting a little monster to stick up its head from beneath a chip and have a good look around.

Longreach came into view and we passed where Quantas was first founded and John Travolta kept one of his planes. This was another town which had suffered every known plague and setback from rabbits to mice, kangaroos and cyclones, droughts and feral dogs. You half wondered it was still there but still there it was, a colourful mishmash of banks and shops with even a nice little cinema at the end of the street. I read in the local newspaper that they'd still got real problems with feral dogs who were attacking the cattle. The government was being urged to spend a lot of money - which it claimed it didn't have - to fence them off.

We often saw kangaroos hanging around the gardens in Longreach eating the flowers and driving the locals bonkers but the government still forbids any sort of cull and consequently the kangaroo population around Longreach has more than doubled in the past three years.

***

However, the quality of the food did improve enormously here, thanks to Elvis Presley – otherwise known as Steve Kelleher – and those who ran the local riverboat cruises.

We decided to try a Thai dinner on offer on the site where we were camping and no sooner had we started on the satay than the fattest Elvis impersonator I have ever seen – even fatter than the original – complete with rhinestone cowboy outfit and sequinned cape – began taking us through all those golden oldies. Steve had a terrific voice which really did sound like the real Elvis, and he sang with the same buttock-clenching fervour, although he did have the worrying habit of getting so carried away with his own singing he kept sticking his microphone into his eye and pretending he had knocked himself out.

But I got even more worried when he started caressing the women who were in raptures in his audience. One rather elderly woman actually made a grab for him as he got into Love Me Tender and that wasn't so bad except her husband didn't even stop chewing his dinner as she did so. When another woman was treated to Elvis's copious touches she, far from being upset, kept laughing uproariously in toothless glee.

Not that our Elvis seemed to care who he felt up and the blokes began getting it too and we were all laughing and smiling as if we'd all had a long night on the happy juice.

***

The next evening was as lovely as a field of freshly opened poppies when a local guide took us down to the river to cruise into the sunset. At first sight the boat, a converted cattle barge, didn't look capable of carrying two people let alone the thirty odd of us. I was reminded of that line by Robert Shaw in Jaws who was standing on the aft deck of his boat when he first saw the shark they had been chasing and declared: "We're gonna need a bigger boat."

Our confidence wasn't much helped when the skipper, who looked so muddy he might have been wrestling with crocodiles for the past half an hour, warned us about the possums which occupied each of the boat's heads. "What you must do is sit there and see if you like him and he likes you. If you both decide you like one another it's all right to get on with whatever you want to get on with."

Surprisingly good nibbles were served up on the chugging craft with one side of the river lighting up fiercely in the setting sun and a thick darkness already beginning to settle on the other. The colours of the sky kept changing, from gold to purple and to a light blue again. Then darkness settled over the whole river and strange birds gave strange calls to the ending of another brilliant Australian day. Then, with a huge explosion of golden light in the far distant woods, the sunset was all over.

We were served a bush meal around a camp fire – a stew with bread and butter. I had loved the Thai dinner when Elvis was crooning to us but this one had to be the best and tastiest meal we'd had since we left Sydney. Even Peninsular and Oriental's finest couldn't have competed with this one and, as I finished it greedily, I reflected that all you need to cook a real meal is for it be hot, fresh and done with a lot of love. Nothing to it really as all those munchkins who are now serving up their deep-fried slops in their roadhouses should work out for themselves before we all start making our own spam sandwiches to feed ourselves and they all go bust.

11: A stick insect gets the ride of its life

The town of Winton's claims to be recognised in the twenty first century were none too clear. Waltzing Matilda was written there by someone called Banjo and dinosaurs roamed around these parts millions of years ago. They are still digging up fossilised dinosaur crap here and claiming another big breakthrough in the long history of fossilised dinosaur crap.

There was a shop in the high street where a rather pathetic, if not arthritic, dinosaur diorama had been built out of plastic and, in the all-you-never-wanted-to-know section about wool Rolf Harris was singing along to a video about unhappy sheep being sheared. Hadn't the miserable old woman who took the money at the door learned what had happened recently to Rolf in London?

No, she had not. It was nothing to do with her and anyway she had always liked him and his voice. I really hate it when you make a little joke and they take it extremely seriously.

The road out of Winton immediately began describing a completely new circle in hell with huge yellowing acres of shrub stretching out to every horizon with many blackened trees that had died in this, the third long season of drought on the bounce. Not even the rain – if it were ever to come – would revive these trees now.

Dark red termite hills dotted the landscape like sand castles on a busy holiday beach. At first I saw only a couple but later hundreds of them appeared then thousands and quite possibly millions. There were also the wonky black crucifix shapes of telegraph poles lining the road, and about a dozen men laying a long red cable. They were prospecting for oil and gas, I was told. You can only get so far on old dinosaur crap. The beds of all the creeks – including the Half Pint Creek – were still parched and cracked.

The odd passing road train made every joint of our rig shake and rattle while, after a few hours or so, I was amused to find myself fantasising about coming across a McDonalds out here in the parched Bush with those huge yellow arches just hanging in a shimmering heat haze. With lips swollen and delirious with thirst I would stagger through the doors and all the cowboys would look up at me as I shouted: "Big Macs all round and fries and large Cokes. And don't you all go worrying about getting fat."

Maybe the heat was getting to me.

We were meeting up with the Grey Nomads in some numbers, all travelling north at this time of year, hoping to escape the winter in the south which, even in golden Australia, can be surprisingly cold and wet. The search for the sun guided almost every move the nomads made. None studied the weather forecasts more avidly and wherever they decided the best weather was, that's where they went.

By now I was managing to unpack a lot more of their story, discovering that there are no fewer than half a million of them involved in what might well be this country's most significant change. They were all looking for a new pleasant way of life at the end of theirs.

Their stories may even herald the way Australia is evolving, I thought, something which may even have a relevance to other countries who are wondering what to do with their old. We have always looked to the young and hippy to make such statements but, in this story, the old were acting out new ideas, with a desire for a new life and an absolute refusal to step forward and guzzle the national swill. Their reasons for breaking away were many and various, as we have already discovered, although, mundanely enough, the main reason seems to be economic insofar as it is a good deal cheaper to support yourself on the road – and almost always in days of brilliant sunshine – rather than in your own home where, of course, it can be painfully expensive just to sit there looking out the window at the rain, hoping someone might call.

***

I had met two Kiwis, John and Debby, in Longreach and they were just completing three years on the road with no end in sight. They loved just about everything about their new way of life and Debby had kept a detailed account of their expenditure – which included site fees, food and petrol – and showed they needed $1,000 to $1,200 a week. They didn't drink alcohol but John managed to spend an astonishing $15 a day on coffee, an expense that clearly irked the beautiful Debby who only ever drank water.

Yet if the coffee bill ever got too high they could always work their passage along with many other Grey Nomads. There were jobs everywhere. In the casinos of Darwin, for example, or picking strawberries or even rounding up cattle.

I met Chris Foley on a free camp, the Apex, outside Longreach, and he told me the most hair-raising stories about his short life as a cattle herder - which, he said on reflection, could well have been a good deal shorter. He had been a technician by trade in Victoria who offered his services to a cattle rancher and next thing he was riding a motorbike around the Bush, rounding up cattle. One of the young steers had fallen behind the main herd and Chris had to get him back to the rest. "Just deliver it and don't hang around," the rancher told him. "Those bulls can become very dangerous if you mess around with their little ones."

Chris got the youngster on to his handlebars and drove him back to the herd. When he got there two bulls began menacing him so he dropped the steer and drove off so fast his backside might have been on fire. But the bulls decided to attack the rancher instead who had been watching everything from what he thought to be a safe distance and got a good goring, ending up in hospital.

The real problem for the modern Grey Nomad is that he is often perceived as a gypsy, seen by many as a thief and sponger who want everything for nothing and no effort. However these nomads are keen to show they do have money, which they are willing to spend, and many businesses are now taking a bigger interest in the Grey Dollar.

Danny Mackay, who I met in Roma, had been on the road for three years in his converted bus on which there was the touching sign: The Two of Us. Grey Nomads always seem to have sound marriages, which is almost vital to survive together in a small space over a long, very bumpy time, Danny told me. He also described the Nomads' attempts to prove their worth in the community.

On one recent camp in Cairns, he said, 200 Grey Nomads kept receipts for all their purchases. These receipts, which were later put on public display, showed that the Grey Nomads had spent $80,000 in Cairns over two days which adds up to an awful lot of Vegemite.

The Nomad numbers are steadily rising too. One of the big rig manufacturers, Alco, is now pushing out a new rig every eleven minutes and they are all selling. Surprisingly few told me they were going on the road because they feared the growth of crime in the city – as the man with the missing tooth once had in Macquarie - although one did point out that crime had spread into the smaller towns, largely because of drugs. A few nomads even put dog kennels near their rigs, even if there were no dogs to go in them. Most of them carried baseball bats to defend themselves if necessary.

When Liz and I were queuing to make a cash withdrawal in Stockton a man told us that someone had tried to blow up the machine only the previous week but they hadn't gotten away with any money. You can see the problem reflected in every shop window in Stockton where there are often signs like: No cash is kept in this store overnight.

As I chatted around I did pick up a few early worries for these old and vulnerable nomads who perhaps need better looking after. I didn't enjoy our last free camp at all. None of us had much sleep because there were a dozen helmeted motor bikers roaring round and round the huge empty space there all night, as if rehearsing for a scene in Mad Max. I wouldn't say they were physically menacing us but they did keep us awake for a good few hours when we needed to be asleep. Certainly we were all gone at first light and few of us seemed to have plans for returning.

Yet the great bonus of being on the road, I believe, is that it might well give you your health back. I once had a doctor friend who always said that good health is ninety five per cent good feelings and I'm already feeling a lot better than when I started out. The road can even mend a breaking heart as I learned when talking to Pat, my newest friend, in Mount Isa.

Pat lost his wife 20 years ago and still hasn't recovered, becoming a nomad and taking off in his van every year from

Sydney to Darwin. There he does a lot of nothing in the sunshine and just sits there thinking about her. The pain is still there but the road helps him to manage it. She would be happy about what he was doing, he believed, particularly if he managed to feed himself properly.

I don't know how I would manage if I lost Liz. I would certainly become a Grey Nomad continually cruising the roads and back lanes of Oz until I found the final end of the final road and was no more. And that would probably come sooner than later because I wouldn't have the faintest clue how to cook anything or feed myself properly. I can't even make toast without burning it to a cinder.

***

Today we drove into the Northern Territories after a night parked up on the side of the Barkly Highway hearing only the deafening roar of the road trains, some as loud as aeroplanes as they roared through my dreams every half an hour or so.

Thus far we have enjoyed almost every aspect of our journey through Australia although I could have done with fewer insects whose sheer nastiness can still make my eyebrows disappear straight into my hairline. This morning we had filled up with petrol and, fortified by a few toasted cheese sandwiches in the roadhouse, returned to the rig only to find a giant stick insect sitting on the windscreen wipers. I've never seen an insect that big but this one was as long as my arm and there was a definite suicidal air about him as Liz tried to dislodge him so we could get on our way. But he wasn't going anywhere even after we prodded and poked him.

Liz turned on the wipers and all that happened was that he clung on to the rubber blades, going up and down, his big prismatic eyes wide with a delicious terror, like a child on a big dipper. Still he refused to get off and go home to the Bush and a doubtless anxious mother.

I managed to get him off in the end with a rolled up copy of the Outback magazine and he managed to fly, opening up his wings and flying sideways for a few feet before crash landing flat on his back on the road, his spiky legs poking up into the air. He was clearly crook after we'd poked him so much and I wanted Liz to put him out of his misery by running him over but she refused to do that, clearly getting worse than Nathan, taking a good ten minutes to skirt around him.

Insects and other vermin have still been a constant problem on the road and our main difficulty has been keeping them out of the rig. First there were the ants which kept breaking out in swarms in the van - first this hole then that hole - all frantically chasing around doing stupid stuff. But we got on top of them in the end with talcum powder. There also seemed to be a growing problem with flies now we are moving north and they became very serious when we spent the night in McKinlay.

Now everyone interested in exactitude and economy in language can only use one word to describe this town and that word is HOLE.

The library was a tiny corrugated shed with a few books, the police station looked like a part-time knocking shop and the only pub, The Walkabout Creek, was alleged to have been the one used by Crocodile Dundee. We stayed in the grounds of The Walkabout Creek and found that the bar had terrible sexist poems posted over the walls and I spotted a giant cricket trying and failing to scale one of the beer taps behind the bar. He kept falling back into the beer and I recalled that old Max Boyce joke about the man who drowned in a vat of beer in the distillery. "He managed to drown himself in the end but only after dragging himself out three times to have a piss."

The flies were bad inside and outside the pub. They kept going into our eyes, ears and mouths, so, in the end, we wore bushman's nets over our heads as we drank our lemonades. If you ever want to look a complete Pommy knobhead it is recommended you wear one of these while trying to drink something. You put a glass to your mouth and the drink seems to spill everywhere except down your throat.

I thought the claim that Crocodile Dundee used this pub suspicious in the extreme. It only came from another of those poxed Hollywood films after all and I don't think the great crocodile hunter would have drunk his beer with a half-drunk giant cricket thrashing around inside his glass or those terrible sexist poems on the walls.

We had a very early night but were still bothered by insects. Our rig has wire mesh all over the door and window spaces so that you can breathe while keeping away from flies and pests, who get in by hanging around waiting for a door to open but there are also tiny black things that can even get through the mesh and are always attracted to light. They kept turning up when we were in bed reading and only this morning did I discover a cure for them. "You just turn off the light," one of my fellow travellers told me. "They hate darkness and as soon as the light goes off they die."

Oh it's that easy is it? Well, yes it is.

Yes, indeed, there is an awful lot to learn about travelling through the Bush. These insects are tricky for sure but it's up to you to get a good deal trickier.

12: When the Bull tried to kill The Clowns

The termite mounds got bigger and more ambitious as we drove into the Northern Territories. Many were knee-high, others the height of an average man and others really wild creations, cathedrals in progress, as others looked like old women with outsize breasts, all just sitting there, with heads bowed as if in terminal despair that their hopes and dreams had come to this.

The strange nature of all these mounds was also highlighted by the local intelligentsia who have clearly enjoyed dressing them up with jockey caps on their heads, torn knickers and even a donkey jacket with hard hats and sunglasses. I jumped when I spotted one man just sitting in the shrub with a mining helmet on his head and a pick on his shoulder, as if taking a break on his way to work, and I stayed in shock until I worked out it was just another fully dressed termite mound.

These mounds are difficult to destroy and I am told that if you want to build a house in Darwin you must first lay down special pipes under the projected building and agree to pump termite poison into these pipes every five years. Termites will eat anything – lawnmowers, the baby's cot, your favourite chair – and they never seem to need any sleep either. Kick one of the smaller mounds over and they will have it completely rebuilt by the morning.

These mounds are at their eeriest and most compelling in the moonlight – looking like thousands, if not millions, of ruined tombstones which were once laid out like endless cemeteries where the troops on both sides had been buried after an enormous inter-galactic war in which everyone perished and no one knew anyone's name.

***

We had been looking for the Daly Waters pub – said by many, with much justification, to be the most eccentric pub in Australia – and despite our bad experience in that Roma bull ring we ended up watching another small rodeo in the grounds of that pub.

Oh how I love these Aussies - even the ambulance people are so cool. When one of the cowboys was bounced off his bucking bronco and ended up unconscious and face down in the ring it took the ambulance people a good five minutes to saunter over to him to see if he was all right. They looked down at him, loosened his shirt collar, patted his cheek and wandered off again while yet more cowboys tried to get themselves killed as they were tossed up in the air to the whoops of the crowd. Finally someone decided the unconscious one should be moved out of the way and he was dragged out by his feet and left on the other side of the fence where he could still barely stand and kept falling sideways when he tried to stand up. They didn't even give him a paracetamol.

But this odd behaviour was nothing compared to what followed: the bull riding. Here again young cowboys were thrown this way and that in the air and the usual routine was the bulls ran off to the side exit, when they had finished their turn, doubtless relieved to get away from all this noisy cheering mayhem.

The show continued like this until one bull decided he didn't want to play anymore, taking up a position in the middle of the ring after getting rid of the man who had managed to stay on him for all of two seconds, pawing the ground and challenging anyone who came near to watch it. He defied everyone and showed no inclination whatsoever to run off home like a good bull.

The clowns, who are there to distract the bull by running close to him and presenting an easy target, were not having any effect either and it was certainly no laughing matter when the bull actually caught one of the clowns and gave him such a goring he had to be taken straight to hospital.

But the show must go on and all that, so more cowboys joined in the fray and a man on a horse trotted into the ring to try and restore law 'n' order. But the bull now tried to gore the horse and actually drew blood on the side of its belly. Thus the horse became afraid of the bull and started running away from him.

A heifer was produced next, perhaps hopeful of calming the father down, but the bull wasn't having any of that paternal guff either and, while going one way, turned sharply and caught the other clown who was also stretchered off to hospital. There were now about ten people in the ring, two on horseback and two on stretchers and carted off to hospital, with another horse injured, all trying to bully the bull into going home to his shed.

But he didn't want to go to his shed so then the star of the show came out, a tiny brown dog who clearly had bigger balls than this bull because he went straight for the bull and tried to bite his eye out. This trick had worked yesterday, I heard, because the dog had hung on to the bull's eye – even when it had been swung all over the place – and, half-blinded and demoralised, the bull had simply given up and gone home as he had long been urged.

But this trick didn't work today and the dog made a mistake in his fancy footwork only for him to get a good mauling too. The dog ran out of the ring and refused to come back in again. It was all a bloody and bleeding mess and had gone on for a good half an hour before a huge cowboy in a red shirt wandered into the ring and took up a position in the middle of it directly facing the bull who was busy snorting and pawing the ground getting ready to charge.

The cowboy was carrying a huge whip which he whirled around a bit before bringing it down with such a loud crack it shook all my fillings loose. The bull immediately left the ring at a good hundred mile an hour closely followed by his heifer.

So after two hospitalisations, an injured horse and a humiliated dog - who has now probably got a thing about bulls which stops him doing any more work with them - we, the crowd, were only left with one question – why didn't they send in the bloody man with the bloody whip in the first place?

***

Daly Waters was one of those blink-and-you'll-miss-it kind of places. The population has never actually exceeded three figures and stood at around six when we got there including a rather strange Scot, Ted, with a big, black beard and a wild mop of hair who rode around on a rackety bicycle with a teddy bear on its handlebars jamming people on to the campsite with ruthless precision, even shouting at some of them for straying a foot over where he had first decreed they should be. He had been here for thirty years but still spoke in the same impenetrable Scottish accent that all Scots retain even after a lifetime of living abroad. He was a bit of a romeo too, I heard, although in all his thirty years here he had never met a woman that desperate. Or it might just have been they didn't understand what he was saying when he was trying to hit on them.

Nothing much happens in the high street of Daly Waters. A tumbleweed may once have blown slowly through the odd dust storm and ants were busy everywhere I looked. However there was one huge drama back in 1969 when two men fought a gun duel here over a woman. One was duly shot and crawled into the nearby garden leaving a trail of blood everywhere until he lay down next to the water sprinkler and died.

This strange, lonely place of termites and flies did play a part in the Second World War although you could write an account of all that on the back of a postage stamp. They built an airstrip here which became the base for the Australian and American bomber raids on the Japanese. The trouble was they rarely had any of the old exploding stuff to rain down on the Japanese, but what they did discover was that they could – allegedly – scare the life out of the Japanese with empty beer bottles of which, unsurprisingly, given where we were, they had stacks and stacks.

When the bottles fell from the bombers, it turned out, they screamed louder than attacking Stukas and, oh boy, did they make a loud bang on impact. Allegedly.

***

There was a small shop opposite the pub on the high street which ran a book exchange and sold T-shirts. Perched precariously on top of its corrugated roof was a wreck of a helicopter with everything hanging off it – or plain broken. The only other commercial activity in the high street was an art gallery which seemed to be built out of odds and sods like most of the buildings in the area. You will be familiar with this school of architecture: throw a bit of this on top of a bit of that and, with any luck, you might well end up with something which might stay up, keep you dry and you can live in. Might.

The owner of this place and artist in residence was Kevin Rogers JP who was opening today, for the first time this season, and we were his first visitors.

Kevin wasn't too happy, as it turned out, since a frog had fallen into his Indian ink and proceeded to crawl all over some of his original paintings causing a mess which was going to take him ages to put right.

He was many things was Kevin, a pure joy to be with, generous with his time and thoughts, and a genius with his paint brush.

He thought the nomads were pretty much all old farts who kept buying expensive rigs which they knew nothing about and didn't have a clue what to do with them. He had once run a caravan site in Western Australia, he said, and you wouldn't believe what kind of idiots came wandering into his office there. "One came in and asked if we could do something about the wind. Can something be done to slow it down or stop or make it go another way? Another complained that his chicken was too big for his oven and another said I was clearly using the wrong kind of electricity on the site."

Certainly Kevin seemed to know all kinds of fascinating stuff like how you can download a mosquito repellent app. to your tablet, and another to set up a high-pitched whine to stop dogs barking. This man could talk for Australia and in all the time he kept talking – maybe five hours non-stop – I don't think he uttered one boring sentence.

The famous Daly Waters pub over the road was rather like most English pubs insofar as the dining room was full of foul language and squealing children running riot under the tables. But there the similarity ended because the main bar itself was like nothing else you have ever fallen over in. Ever.

Hundreds of torn and grubby knickers and brassieres hung over the bar counter and almost every wall was festooned with baseball caps, hundreds of banknotes from all over the world, motoring badges and personalised drink holders. The T-shirts in particular had the usual sexist ravings on them: "My wife says it's either her or fishing. I'm sure going to miss her."

The toilets say: SHEILAS or BLOKES.

Oh how we laugh.

One pole was festooned with hundreds of flip-flops, or thongs as they call them out this way, although you did worry about the cleanliness of the place when you noticed that all these thongs were covered in cobwebs suggesting there were more spiders inside them than there were termites in the Bush.

There was some entertainment over dinner in the dining room in which a Bushie with a long, grey beard sang songs about hard life was in the Bush with a voice which sounded like a rope under a door. This one could have had a bright and profitable career working for the London Council evicting squatters. Everyone knows you can't beat up squatters but, after one song from this man, all of them would have been running down the street with their hands clamped over their ears. Indeed he did pretty much end up emptying the dining room with his tuneless drones, leaving a small group of about eight of us, shivering with the blasts of cold air sent by the huge fans in the roof above.

I suspect these few remaining punters were not only freezing cold but stone deaf as well.

13: Hunting Crocodiles in the Billabong

We were sitting on a bench in Kakadu in the Northern Territories waiting for a bus which would take us hunting crocodiles. The sun, yet again, had come up in a brilliant blaze of blue sky and the birds all around were staging a somewhat belated dawn chorus.

But, unlike the sweet songs of most awakening birds, this chorus was a terrible racket barely warranting an E for effort. One bird kept sighing as if he was on his death bed with barely five minutes left to live, another made a sharp crack as in whip, and there was the occasional harsh squawk as in parrot, all of them devoid of grace or subtlety. Cockatoos start when everyone else has finished and they make a worse racket than all the others put together. These cockatoos can't even fly properly. They fly up into the air and seem to lose control of their wings before crashing, as if just shot, down to the ground.

I've been having an unsuccessful time with wildlife lately and even my first encounter with a snake – a python at that - was a bit of a farce barely worth mentioning. In Katherine our television aerial decided to fall apart so we got a local repair guy, Terry, to fix it. He agreed to do this and the usual Aussie pantomime happened: five minutes to fix it and about an hour to tell his life story.

He's got a farm, he said, and only last week his wife spotted a big python in the yard so she told him to take it to the local waste dump and dispose of it. He did as he was told and the people in charge of the dump told him to take it to the back of the tip where the snake will be really happy – and maybe live forever - feeding on rubbish. There was no question of killing the thing: everyone wants the python to start a new life on the rubbish tip where it will be really well fed and happy. It's that Aussie thing again: they really do seem to love anything and everything that moves or crawls or slithers. There was simply a natural bond there.

But there was a twist because yesterday Terry's wife spotted a baby python out in the yard and, certain that the big python they had put on the tip was in fact the mother, she thought that Terry should take it to be with its mother so they could be together again and be happy and well fed on the rubbish dump. Terry was on his way there when he had the call to fix our television aerial. We could see the baby python if we wanted. Our first snake! We could see our first snake which Terry kept in his van in a sack.

But it was a big disappointment, small and barely moving, not worth picking up even if that was what I was invited to and declined as graciously as possible.

But the little one is anyway now back with his mother on the rubbish dump so this is one Bush story with a happy ending.

So we were not doing too well on the wild animal front and things didn't improve now we are in Kakadu, being savaged by mosquitoes who gave Liz a real roughing up the previous night. Liz also had problems with the platoons of frogs which hung around the camp lavatory. You have to tread very carefully before going in there particularly at night since they are always waiting for the door to open and love whatever it is inside. There are signs on all doors warning us to keep all such doors closed.

So it didn't augur well for us as we wait for a bus to take us hunting crocodiles. We needed the crocs to be big and frightening and I needed something to write about, not that pitiful little python or all those pointless, burping frogs. I wanted a big croc to explode out of the water and eat my notebook with its big jaws. That would make a good headline. Crocodile delivers critical verdict on hack's useless notes and eats the lot – Biro, hand and all.

The bus came and about ten of us piled on. As we were driven away we were overwhelmed by the forests all around. It was still the rainy season and we ran through a deep flood on the road before stopping outside a long caged path – The Rage Cage - which was there to protect us from any croc attacks, they said, as we boarded our boat. These crocs were everywhere at this time of year and desperate to eat anything they could get their jaws into, even us, we kept being told. But I'm sure all this scary talk was just to put the wind up us, which it did.

Yet what did happen - as we cruised silently out into the billabong – was that all my petty resentments, fears and frustrations drained straight out of my legs as we beheld the fulminating beauty and grandeur all around. We were completely silenced by it: the great grass plains being swept and stroked by breezes and the watery tracts covered by thousands of white and blue water lilies, all in full bloom. A fire hawk stood guard on one of the dead trees gazing down on us as we moved past and, further out again, a bird with a red head, a jacana, was walking on water. This trick had earned him the appropriate name of the Jesus bird. When it took off it had a drooped tail and a head held high, rather like the shape of the old Concorde.

We moved into Alligator Creek on the Yellow River and a fine white-bellied sea eagle was sitting on a large branch tearing at the body of a catfish and enjoying himself mightily. These eagles were the boss birds hereabouts and were only ever challenged by other eagles. This can lead to a furious, extremely bloody fight in which they lock talons and spiral around in the air until they fall together into the river where one will try to drown the other.

Two of these battling eagles landed in front of this craft only last week, were were told, and, when the one was on the point of succeeding in drowning the other, a crocodile moved in and finished them both off. Crocodiles like eating eagle but rarely get the opportunity to grab hold of one since eagles are strong fliers and usually put up too much of a fight.

No crocodiles just yet, as it happened, but that hardly mattered. The company which runs these cruises never guarantee you'll see one and always refuse when anyone asks for their money back in the event of a crocodile no-show. This is a tour of the wetlands which has the biggest variety of birds in Australia, they argue, even if they do admit using a huge croc, with the sun glistening on its back, in their advertising.

A kingfisher flew past in an unforgettable and unmistakable blur of blue. I was still overwhelmed by everything. Everywhere I looked made me want to get down on my knees and the presence of God was already stirring somewhat ominously inside me as I saw vague black figure walking through a heat haze as in a mirage. God had been looking after us on this trip for a while now, and I knew that an angel watching over us from the top of our rig was real. We kept drifting through sticky situations on this trip with a suspicious ease and, despite this challenging countryside, neither of us had yet felt one moment of fear.

In the distance there was a brumby, a wild horse, wading, chest-deep, in the waters. Crocs will also go for one of these if they are hungry enough and the water is the right depth for them to work in and drown the horse with their death rolls. A few will even team up if necessary to take a horse down. Crocs live off everyone and everything.

And then it happened, silently and darkly, without a murmur or shout. A pair of cloudy yellow eyes with black slits was looking up at us. Up came a spiny hard head and the long corrugated serrations of the back of a huge croc calmly floating along next to us, those cold eyes clamped straight on me and watching my every move.

I have always enjoyed zoos and have visited most of the major ones in the world where I have seen plenty of crocs in captivity. But this was a special moment, being out here in the wild places where he lives and hunts, moving along the billabong as our guide warned us sternly not to stick our arms over the boat's rail or we might lose something useful. Not that my croc looked as if he might do something like that, it must be said. He was being pretty cool about everything, as was I.

These crocs can pick up tremors of something interesting, which might also be good to eat, from a few hundred yards away. They are supreme killing machines who will swim anywhere for any distance if there might be a good feed on offer. This is a two-million-year-old survivor who has the most effective kit for moving around land and water in the world; he was even around at the time of dinosaurs - and look what happened to dinosaurs.

He disappeared as swiftly and silently as he had emerged leaving a trail of fine bubbles as he looked for somewhere comfortable on the riverbed to spend a cool hour or so in the morning heat. Lucky crocodile. I only wish I could be down there with him. Many of our group were practically expiring in the heat, not much helped by the odd cooling breeze which did occasionally find us. But my croc was far better equipped for diving deep than us; when he goes under he can reduce his heart rate to one beat every fifteen minutes.

We cruised on marvelling at the huge lotus lilies growing at the edge of the fields of tall grass. Small birds darted in and out of the mangrove branches. Dragonflies zipped everywhere – zip, zip, zip. Occasionally the head of a little turtle would bob up. Those big trumpet leaves of the lotus lilies can be used to carry water, we were told. You can even cook with these leaves. On another tree a tiny golden tree snake was mooching around looking for food. Every living thing out here was looking for food and I could feel God taking a great pleasure in the savage beauty of his primal creation. What we saw all around us was indeed a masterpiece which could not be improved on in any detail.

We came across another crocodile having a nap on the edge of more reed beds where egrets were standing around staring into space. But this croc didn't even open his eyes as we moved closer. We were there for around five minutes when the croc did wake up and we were all eyeballing one another until he clearly decided he'd had enough and disappeared beneath a cloud of bubbles. Pretty boring really, not at all like my first croc, who I was now missing quite badly.

Our trip was finally over and my faith in the way this wonderful country kept surprising me had been fully restored. Me and my croc are going to be an item for a good while yet and whenever I think about him, which is quite lot, I hope to see him again soon when we will meet on a date at the same time at the usual place on the first reed bed on the left in the billabong.

Yet far more exciting for me – even more exciting than the first appearance of the croc – is the sense that God really was back in my life again, not as an aggressive, noisy force, beating me senseless and leaving me to start again, as happened in Malaysia, but as a calm contemplative force, replete with the beauty of his own matchless creation, who was going to protect us throughout our journey rather like a favourite uncle who was more than happy to protect and watch over us until the end of our days.

This belief was not only provoked by the savage grandeur of the billabong but also by the certainty that we had gone back to the beginning of things as they were millions of years ago. And that black figure in the shimmering heat haze might have had significance too. Oh sure he might merely have been an intensification of a desire most of us will have from time to time – to see the Christ figure walking again on this earth – but that figure also told us, I thought, about God's most persistent and greatest promise that, when the time is right, he will come back and rescue us all from this great and dark storm of evil which is now gathering so thickly over the world.

Yes, everything is quiet and still in the billabong today. But so too is the eye of a storm.

14: The Most Gorgeous Market in the World

We finally hit Darwin, the most northern city in Australia and were greeted by heavy showers, our first rains for months. At this time of the year the seasons are on the cusp between wet and dry and odd things happen which are something and nothing. As the rain falls the temperature rises. The mozzies get busier too – even by their normal busy standards - and even seem able to get Liz in the dark which suggests they know something about night navigation which would be of interest to the Royal Air Force.

The snakes are also up and about in this strange in-between time of the year and there were signs around the campsite warning you to watch out for them. Not the ideal companions for any holiday you might say and you might be right.

In truth the site owners were more worried by the non-appearance of the Grey Nomads. Where are they? Last year at this time they are all up here in their thousands. Many had to park out in the street and wait until they were telephoned when a vacancy occurred. Maybe the nomads worried about the changing weather more than we do.

Darwin was a huge surprise: a vibrant modern city, alive with bottle shops and fast food outlets which reminded me of Dubai with its big Malls where you can eat almost anything you want, particularly South East Asian food. Many families from Indonesia and Malaysia have settled here in Darwin serving up their tantalising dishes in cardboard containers with plastic knives and forks.

Darwin civic centre, with its precise new buildings, looked as if it had all been finished yesterday. You can see how seriously they take tourism by the sheer size of the Information Centre with piles of leaflets about everywhere you may want to visit as well as four desks where newly arrived visitors queue to work out a Plan A for their holidays with the mozzies. We may remember almost the whole of the city was torn apart, if not flattened, by Cyclone Tracy in Christmas 1974. All newly built houses now have safe rooms which can withstand any new cyclone. All you need do is sit in there and wait for the cyclone to run out of puff. In the museum you could stand in a rather rickety shed which was shaken around as if in a cyclone and it was so convincingly scary we hung on to one of the railings in there for dear life hoping we would manage to escape.

But Darwin was a good place to live, I thought, and vaguely remembered that Ronnie Biggs, one of the great train robbers, had also chosen to live here when he was out on the lam after breaking out of Wandsworth prison in London. I dug around in the story a bit and discovered that Biggs received plastic surgery before coming to Darwin and had chosen Australia because they also spoke English here. He certainly sat well in the line of the other English convicts who had first come here and founded Australia even if his crime was quite big by any standards and those of the original forced settlers were hardly anything at all. A couple of chickens indeed.

Charmian, his wife, and their children joined him here but took flight down to Melbourne when it looked as if they were about to be rumbled.

Biggs was on the run for more than 30 years only to be betrayed be a reporter from the Daily Express. But what would he expect from a reporter from the Daily Express? You would have to be mad to trust anyone from that rag.

***

Last night we went to perhaps the most gorgeous market in the world on nearby Mindil Beach. The stalls were all spread out on the grass along the edge of the sand where everyone paused at around seven o'clock to watch the sun drop down from the sky and into the ocean. I have been to markets in Australia before – and was particularly fond of the one in Byron Bay - but Mindil was something else, more a party than a place for flogging cheap stuff where we were greeted by a drum 'n' bass band at the entrance together with a five-horned didgeridoo. These mesmerising sounds can get right into your blood like speed and shake everything about a bit.

There were also displays of fire-eating, a sort of theatre of whips and a most beguiling girl, beautiful and sinuous, who was doing things you never thought possible with a hulahoop, getting the thing to move up and down the length of her body while she moved around inside it and all to the throb of drum 'n' bass. The strange thing was she was almost alone in not trying to make any money from her whirling gig.

But nothing could quite prepare you for the actual sunset when around a thousand of us crowded down on to the sand to watch Mother Nature's daily star turn which put all the other acts here in the market in the shade. This dying sun put on a display of stupendous, fiery exuberance, which penetrated almost every corner of the market making everything shimmer and dance with an orange hue. The whole display clawed at your eyes and touched the deepest parts of your heart. No matter how many times you saw it you would never tire of these sensational Mindil sunsets, particularly the afterglow when the huge orange slashes turned purple and black while the clouds kept moving around as if they were wondering how best they could fit into the whole painting.

Later that night I dreamed of that sunset and heard again the mesmerising drone of that didgeridoo calling this lovely land home.

The stalls sold mostly food but there were many busy with art, books and clothes and, as I continued walking around them, I was lucky enough to bump into Monte Dwyer, a writer of the Bush like no other, here flogging his own books. He has written a fine study of the Grey Nomads saying that they might be the most significant movement of people in this part of the world since the Gold Rush. He was a personable, friendly bloke, decently dressed and strangely good looking.

He insisted he had long gone mad and he was certainly unlike some of the other Bushies I had met, wandering around the spinifex with the arse of their pants hanging out and the wildest dreadlocks shaking around as they kept muttering the truth of their madness.

Rather strangely Monte used to be a weather forecaster – a telly face! – before he moved into the Bush, writing four in his Red in the Centre series about the post war baby boomers who are retiring from the cities and going for a long, never-ending drive in the Bush. He had always been interested in the Grey Nomad story, he told me, and quizzed them about all manner of things from whether they ever stole anything from campsites to their sex lives. He didn't get far on the sex issue of course, largely, you suspect, because, at their age, there isn't anything worth answering questionnaires about.

This movement is bound to grow and grow, he says. What we are seeing is the most cashed-up generation in our history now enjoying a carefree long holiday in the world's largest theme park or retirement village. It will also lead to fundamental changes in our society.

But will it help the Aborigines?

Monte's not really sure but, as we all know, the older we get the less certain we become about everything. But he does think the nomads may yet be of help to the Aborigines precisely because these same nomads in their RVs are busy trying to reconnect to their roots, be they Aboriginal or European.

This is a very exciting insight, I thought, insofar as the nomads, with all their skills and experience of life, might be precisely the ones who could introduce the alienated Aborigines into the Aussie dream by exposing them to new ideas which will bring the two sides together. Something must be done and these people should not be abandoned.

Do the nomads, who have a lot in common with the Aborigines, hold the key? Can the nomads supply the final missing piece of the Aussie jigsaw? Who knows? I don't – and neither does Monte - but it's something I'm going to continue to dig around in.

You can tell the Grey Nomads are well versed in life skills just by the state of their legs which are always on show because they all wear shorts in the heat. They've got their big expensive rigs with showers, microwaves and stuff through sheer hard work, you can work out, just by the gnarled state of their legs which are all shapes with bones sticking out where they shouldn't be sticking out, knee caps which are anything but the shape of normal knee caps and many of the veins missing where they have been stripped out by surgeons for by-passes.

So what with all that, not to mention their deformed, bunioned feet, many of the nomads manage to look as if they have been bombed or shot at in some terrible Bush war and no surgeon has ever bothered to dig out the stray shrapnel. You wonder how many of them manage to stand up at all let alone walk but they do and what is more they all seem pretty cheerful while also perhaps proving that hard work never killed anyone but it sure makes a hell of a mess of them.

Those legs in their fancy rigs also tell you that Australia is essentially a working class country where the rewards are high for those who do work hard. In this country you do always get a chance and it's all down to you to make the most of it.

15: "Them we loves and them we hates."

I kept thinking Australia might even have lost its ability to amaze but yesterday I met a million reasons why I was dead wrong yet again.

Liz was keen to cruise along the Katherine Gorge in Nitmiluk National Park but I wasn't. I've never been keen on rocks no matter how they are piled up. A little rock always goes a long way in my book. You can't eat rocks, play with them or even sleep with them. A rock is a rock is a rock.

Anyway Liz got me down to where the boats are tied up and I stood for a while gazing up at a high tree outside the visitors' centre which was like nothing else I have ever seen. There were huge brown pendants hanging off its branches all wrapped in brown canvas sheets which occasionally fluttered but not with the wind. There was also a fair bit of screeching going on in this tree when a few of these pendants took to alarmed flight with their translucent wings catching the sun.

What I was looking at was a large gathering of flying foxes – or fruit bats – all hanging off this tree – and the next and the next. There may have been a million of them, one of the park rangers told me. He added that they weren't settled here and he just wished they would go somewhere else. These flying foxes damage almost everything they get near although they do help the eco-system by spreading seeds in the torrential downpours of their dumps. What these foxes do when they want to spend a penny is turn their bodies around as they hang on their branches, spread their wings wide and dump over everyone and everything. These dumps can change the colour of cars and this is why the Aussies, who are forever cleaning and polishing their cars, hate them so much. There are indeed some who love these flying foxes but a lot more who hate them.

But they are not easy to move on. A huge mob once settled on the botanic gardens in Melbourne and many of the city's great and good, doubtless fearing for the colour of their wretched cars, wanted them shot. They didn't get far with that proposal but, at huge expense, it was decided to truck them up to Queensland, release them in a forest and hope they would settle there. But on their release these flying foxes managed to get back to Melbourne well before the truckers.

On our own travels we thought we had caught up with them in Mataranka where they once lived above a natural spring by day and went out foraging for food by night, coming back in a black swarm at sunrise. The authorities wanted them out and those who were using the famous natural springs for a health cure were fed up with being dumped on too. The place had clearly become somewhere where you went for a cure and risked going home with an incurable disease.

Their solution was to erect a water sprinkler system in the surrounding palms at Mataranka and the foxes, fed up with being constantly showered, took off one night and never returned.

It wouldn't be so bad, I guess, except the foxes are really, really ugly with their upturned Dracula teeth and flat faces which suggest they have just been French kissing one of those Australian road trains. So it can't be long before the authorities find an effective way of moving them on from here in Katharine too.

I didn't think we would see much that was interesting on our trip down the gorge and, after meeting up with the extremely interesting flying foxes, that's how it worked out. There was nothing going on anywhere, perhaps because it was so hot and everyone might have been given a day off. We had been promised all kinds of thrills on this trip up the gorge – Aboriginal art, wild crocs, flowers and rare birds – but all we saw was an empty cage which, we were told, the rangers use to trap salt-water crocs – who can be very dangerous – and who would then be carted off somewhere safe.

The rangers keep an eye on the salties which are difficult to kill if they get too boisterous. Salties have even been known to attack people in their 'tinnies' or fishing boats and have even, allegedly, eaten their engines and propeller blades. The only real way to kill a mad saltie, we were told, was with a nice big shotgun. "All you have to do is push it straight down the gator's throat and give it both barrels."

The Aboriginal art on one of the cliffs in Katherine consisted of a small circle which may have been a man's head and a few red blotches which suggested an artistic botch-up. Most of this creation was covered with tree foliage although it must be said that the authorities could have easily improved the quality of the art merely by introducing a lot more tree foliage.

In two hours of cruising not only did we not see one croc but not one bird. We were taken into a cave at the end of the second gorge and promised we would see fairy martins building nests in there having just returned from East Timor but we gazed up at the cave roof and saw nothing since the birds had yet to find their way home from East Timor and their nests had yet to be built.

At seventy nine dollars a head I thought this trip pretty useless although we were all greeted, when we got back, by the same swarm of flying foxes which even now the authorities are planning to get rid of. They are the only really interesting feature in that gorge and they were planning to get rid of them!

They may be ugly and they may dump on Aussie cars but they certainly did touch something deep in my Welsh soul like so many other natural emblems of this strange, vivid and savage country, which is so packed with such wonderful emblems I often feel I am walking through the pages of the Bible and I am increasingly wondering if this might even be a new Promised Land where our Man of Sorrows will return.

What I am seeing out here seems to be increasingly pointing in that direction. I have made many trips to the Holy Land as a journalist and they were always talking of his return there on the plains of Armageddon but I don't see that at all. I see him appearing out here in the Bush one morning and rubbing his hands together, which will have amazingly long and beautiful fingers, as he decides how he is going to start clearing up this mess.

16: The Worldwide Tracks of my Useless Tears

We are standing on the main street of Wyndham, a long, slightly lost looking town, hanging on the edge of the Joseph Bonaparte Gulf in northern Australia and, with the place hotter than the hobs of hell and well over 100 degrees, I am mortified by guilt about a crime I committed here fifty five years ago.

My crime was about as low as crimes come in this part of the world insofar as I conned an Aborigine out of a stuffed crocodile and today I've come back to the scene of the crime perhaps in the insane hope of making amends to that poor man for stealing his croc or at least to say sorry to someone. In a just world I should have been thrashed for that theft or sentenced to five years hard labour – if not more - down one of the local gold mines.

It is midday and Liz and I have walked down to the new pier and boat ramp where we can look over to a lone cargo ship tied up on Anton's Landing, with another bigger jetty further along the muddy foreshore. That's where the ship I was signed on, the Canopic, a tramp cargo ship, tied up more than fifty years ago. I was a lowly engineer steward and a gang of us went up to the Wyndham Hotel, which is still standing over the road here, to do what we always did after long days just watching the quarrelling waves: get roaring drunk.

I was young and wild, barely seventeen and ready for anything. To this day I am always surprised I survived my youth, as is almost everyone who ever knew me. We all piled into the bar and it was schooners of grog all round and then some more. An Aborigine approached me and asked if I was interested in buying this large stuffed crocodile he was holding. Oh yes I was. He wanted eighty dollars for it – way beyond my means – but I said I had a "Rolex" watch that he might be interested in exchanging for the croc. And he was.

We are outside the Wyndham Hotel, the sun is high and I'm feeling worse than ever. How can anyone steal anything off an Aborigine? It's like murder, something against the natural order of things and, as we go in there for lunch, I half expect him to recognise me and leap on me before beating the hell out of me and shouting how he wanted his stuffed croc back.

Liz needs to use the public toilet and, when she has finished, is rather surprised to discover that she has been widdling over a frog which somehow seems able to perch on the sheer walls of the pan. The frog croaks his pleasure at her and she is so pleased with his response she takes a photograph of him. Nothing seems to surprise us any longer on this journey. We have become so Australianised we are always rather surprised if something normal happens.

We sit down for lunch and I'm sure I recognise the old fans on the ceiling. I remember the local men who sat at that bar and drank until they fell unconscious or their money ran out. If they had any money left when they came to, they drank some more until the cash was gone. They could drink like that for days and even weeks at a time. One wife crawled under the floorboards of the bar and set alight some rags under the spot where she knew her husband was drinking away his wages, managing to scare him into running home to his starving kids before he had drunk the lot.

Wyndham had an extremely lively beginning and got going in 1890 with the Gold Rush but that only lasted a few years. Despite the thousands of hopefuls who turned up they barely dug enough to make a single gold filling. It was always a tough, violent place where competing diggers really did shoot one another. Afghans settled here with their camels and kidnapped the local Aborigine girls for you know what. Dingoes' ears were often used for money as well as shin plasters for IOUs.

The Chinese also came and stayed, still working the stores. A giant meat processing factory was built here in 1919 with cattle herded up through Australia and slaughtered before being packaged and sent off on the ships to Europe. The factory had a blood drain for the bone and offal and hundreds of crocodiles were attracted by the smell of blood, lining up six deep waiting for whatever came out next. That was certainly where my croc – or at least his mother – had come from.

***

Liz and I are eating our lunch and I spot a figure hurriedly crossing the dining room, looking around him anxiously, with a big stuffed crocodile on his shoulder. He has long hair and is dressed in black. Touch me and I'll blow you up, his general demeanour says. Now he is rushing down the rough path to the ship. He has done the deal for the croc but has neglected to tell the Aborigine that he got the "Rolex" for a few pounds on the way out here from an Arab in a canoe in Port Said and it only worked for five minutes or so when vigorously shaken.

Virtually the whole of the ship's company come out on deck to see their long-haired engineer steward carrying a stuffed crocodile up the gangplank on his shoulder. He was not a nice young man this engineer steward. He was a rebel dog full of crazy ideas absorbed from the books, films and plays he'd been devouring ever since he started to read. He was also writing his own great novel on the ship which was very much like all the other stuff he admired – full of violence, perversion and cruelty. In one sense he was a standard bearer for the artistic corruption of his age, although of course he didn't see it that way. That's the very last way he thought of himself.

The next morning the Canopic is due to sail and there is panic on Anton's Landing because the Aborigine had worked out his watch was duff. He wants his croc back and has even got on to the ship, only to be thrown off. The engineer steward was advised to hide with his croc and that's what he did, down in the engine room until the ship had cleared Boney's Gulf.

Yet today he is back with his wife and has got so worked up about his theft he's not much enjoying his lunch. He has made inquiries hereabouts but no one can help. Probably dead they say. Aborigines tend not to last long and this makes him feel worse. If he had paid him in real dollars the poor man might have eaten better and lasted longer.

Everything else in the place is pretty much dead too. The Meat Works has long closed and there is only a lone live crocodile on the foreshore who bullies any other crocs who may come near. Even a local crocodile farm has closed. The Wyndham Hotel where we are sitting is run down and up for sale although Anton's Landing is still in use.

And here I am, an old man in a long, hot season of black rain, with all kinds of things wrong with him, looking down the long corridor of his life, still using words and writing books trying – and usually failing - to make sense of everything. The tracks of my useless tears. Oh yes, those tracks are now running all over the world and there is clearly nothing at all he can now do about any of them.

17: The Crumbling Music of the Breaking Heart of God

The nomad traffic has all been rattling north, making their ways via free lay-bys or roadhouse car parks, mostly to Broome in Western Australia where, we had been told, the season has just begun and four months of untrammelled sunshine bliss awaited.

I don't know why we are all heading to Broome. I for one had never heard of the place until a few months ago but it's clearly the place to go to this year so that's where we are going. Nomads chat about the place incessantly and you keep hearing there's no point in going there unless you've booked because it's always full up. This, like a lot of nomad chatter, turns out to be inaccurate. They often seem to pick up a bit of chatter on the road and embellish it wrongly.

Crocodiles out here will always grab your dog if you are walking too close to a riverbank even if it's on a lead. If you don't get out of the way of a road train it will hit you off the road because it can't brake and stop in time. Otherwise it will clip you and make your rig burst into flames.

We have just passed the giant Kimberley mountain range which rises up on the horizon in great rhapsodies of stone and space. The termite mounds out this way are big and slummocky. There are five different species of termites in Australia, I have learned, who build their homes according to what they eat. The termites in the Kimberleys eat grass which make their mounds look as shapeless as the massive dumps of lost herd of elephants. The more architectural shapes in the Northern Territories are made by termites who eat wood so there's a real balance to their work with fine lines from top to bottom, always pleasing to the eye.

Travelling with nomads can often lead to a complete education in everything since they have picked up all kinds of arcane knowledge on the road, often gleaned from Aborigines. If you get a puncture you can pack the flat tyre with grass. Washing powder can be used for brake fluid. Tree branches can be used as car jacks by tying them to the wheel and rolling it over.

But even the Aborigines have yet to work out how to fix a modern car with computers; they don't even try, which is why the highways are often littered with dead, modern cars since no one anywhere – and that includes the Aborigines - can fix them and it costs a fortune to get them towed in. In one stretch of road we counted nine fairly recent cars just sitting there abandoned, not even worth the trouble or expense of rescuing.

Liz drove carefully around a cow wandering down the centre of the road and, about fifty yards on, there were two eagles sitting on a tree branch watching this cow's slow, erratic path. Aha, I remembered from before what those eagles were up to. They always prefer fresh road kill and so they were just sitting in that tree waiting for one of our rigs to do their dirty work for them.

***

We cut off the Broome road to visit the artist Mark Norval in Derby who, I had been told, had done a lot of wonderful work with the Aborigines. I still hadn't thought of anything sensible to write about the Aborigines but I guessed I didn't need to know much about what they are up to in Derby since I could probably work out a lot of it myself just using my reporter's eyes.

Derby has the usual shops, including a busy Woolworth's supermarket, and sits on the edge of the huge mudflats of King Sound, where high winds and rampaging cyclones would sweep in making all the local animal and insect life come hurrying in to find shelter in the town because they don't like high winds and cyclones either.

The population is largely Aboriginal and I just watched them walking around in groups going about their business which seemed to consist mainly of sitting around for hour after hour in groups outside shops or on the sides of roads. Occasionally they would break up the group and scatter, perhaps into the furthest corners of the car park, where, I was told, they might even shout the most vicious abuse at one another, usually about members of other families. They use the foulest language.

None of them – not even the young – seem to want to wander anywhere except in a group. The groups set off, break up, re-gather and set off again. They are forbidden to drink but most of them do, given any opportunity, and when that happens they are to be seen rolling around the pavement laughing and hitting one another and often drawing blood. I had heard they had recently found a way of making alcohol out of Vegemite, an unlikely brew which made them totally legless for a dollar.

Sometimes they pick up a warning from a passing policeman but such warnings are always ignored or laughed at. I occasionally followed them from a distance but, rather like the rest of Australia, never really understood what they were up to. They really are the most mystifying bunch I've ever come across.

Most of the windows and doors of Derby are grilled or barred and clearly the whole of the white population is scared stiff of the Aborigines. When they decide they really need a drink they will steal anything that moves to get it. There are many decent Aborigines who stay sober and out of the way, I am assured but, as ever, it's the bad boys who always stagger around the middle of the roads or fight one another and get all the attention.

Mark Norval has a gallery here in which he sells Aboriginal and his own magnificent art. He encourages interested local Aborigines to come to work and learn in his gallery. He says you can get everywhere with an Aborigine if you just show him respect but that's not always easy. Only that morning one of his protégés was caught stealing two carved moab nuts although he vehemently denied it. You can see the problems Mark has to deal with but he insists we can't reject them just because they don't think like us. We keep wanting to change them but that's never going to work.

Mark is one of the unsung saints of our time and Australia should put someone like him in charge of Aborigines since he seems to understand these suffering people and knows how to deal with them. Australia must learn how to deal with them too since, from where I stand, a whole heap of trouble is building up precisely because the Aborigines keep being bullied all the time and locked out of their community meeting places or even thrown in the jug for no proper reasons. They are also banned from wherever the whites drink, and can often be seen gazing in over the walls at the whites inside the pubs getting legless. It seems Aborigines just can't take alcohol; it's something in their DNA; drink makes them daft as brushes.

Yet Mark has suffered grievously for his beliefs and work, trying to commit suicide himself a few years back after one of his prize pupils hung himself. That was the fiftieth he had lost in the same way during his career – fiftieth! - and it all became too much for him and he took an overdose. These days he still has to fly down to Perth regularly to be treated for depression.

We purchased one of Mark's huge paintings of a mountain in the Kimberleys and this now hangs on the wall of our bedroom in Bala, here in North Wales, the last thing we see at night before going to sleep and the first thing we look at when we awake in the morning.

It is a mountain such as you have never seen before, the whole high outline of it tinged with bright red which is reflected in the ground at the foot of the mountain. Yet the main body of the mountain stands on coloured oblongs of all shapes and sizes and, if you look at the totality of it long enough, you find yourself becoming delirious with a sort of joy and an overwhelming longing to be back in the arms of this ravishing land once again.

***

Later that night in Derby Liz and I walked down to the huge mudflats to watch the sunset. Near us a group of about twenty young and old Aborigines sat, black on red, chattering amongst themselves in the grass on the edge of the mud. The sun sank into a blaze of red and, for a moment, you could see the blood of the world, the blood of the Lamb, pouring across the fiery sky.

The great Aussie dream can yet turn into an endless wakening nightmare, I believe, unless this country can find a way of dealing with all this, a way of listening to people like Mark who does believe in, and understand, what he is talking about.

God has told us often enough that we should all love one another and die. The Aussies have not found it possible to love Aborigines and that's why they are now dying. They are dying simply because they don't want to be locked out. They need love which, one way and another, we all need.

If Australia found a way of banning the grog for a while, what a great gift that would be to themselves and the lost and wandering Aboriginals. Everyone should learn that alcohol is just a poison that will one day kill you stone dead years before your time.

So I could see and hear a lot of things in that weeping Derby sunset with the Aborigines chattering amongst themselves nearby. I could hear the sharp flutings of a few birds and the roar of distant passing cars. A few frogs were croaking too but most of all I could only hear the crumbling music of the breaking heart of God.

***

At this point my Oz travelogue has reached – what? – about half way and, like most authors, I have been worrying if I will have enough material for a strong middle section which will carry me on to a banging end. I also worry that the book in general will have a decent heft to it, if I can maintain a good narrative drive right through and, most importantly of all, if it can hold the readers' interest.

But there has been an unfolding story behind the writing of this book so far which I have not mentioned merely because I wasn't at all sure that it had any meaning or relevance to what I was trying to do. I now have a way of gauging my readers' interest in any section of this book, I can tell how many have read it and what they think about it. Yes, this book has now become something many people will want to read, I believe, because I'm not now foisting my thoughts on them - as all writers do – since my readers can also foist their thoughts on me. This book will become a mirror reflecting their ideas and thoughts which will also shape mine. Indeed this might even be the first democratic book, certainly the first to be edited and shaped by its readers.

I'd better try and explain this carefully. It was my good friend Noel Carroll of Manly in Sydney who first suggested that I should write this book as a blog. I was very cool about this idea largely because I didn't know what a blog was. Anyway it was easy enough to do since all you did was write the blog a chapter at a time on your computer and then, with the aid of my trusty dongle, post it to the blog address complete with picture. Somehow – and I'm not at all sure how – they put up the picture big with your headline across the top and it always looked good.

It soon became clear that this was a good way of writing my type of book since my normal routine on most of my pilgrimages, say, was to return home with a sack of rubbish – pamphlets, local guide books, notebooks full of my undecipherable handwriting, postcards, bus tickets and anything else that might be relevant to what I was writing about. It would take me a month or two to sort all this out and maybe three months to write up the book. My pilgrimages were always short; my publishers, SPCK, gave me a wodge of money, patted me on the head and the next summer I was ready to go again.

But with a blog, I soon saw, I could write about the events on the road almost as soon as they happened and then post my report straight away. People would read them as I wrote them – we had a poster on the back of our van showing our best rugby player, the mighty George North, running through the Aussie rugby pack. This poster also said we were touring Australia and invited people to follow our journey online and get in touch with us if possible.

(This photograph of George North running through the Aussie pack also has a huge national and symbolic importance for Wales since defeating Australia is seen as almost the sole purpose of the national Welsh rugby team. We don't even dare fantasise about beating New Zealand's All Blacks.)

***

It was a strange experience on a campsite, say, to send off the blog and have someone knocking on your door half an hour later telling you what they thought about it. What they said was always helpful and it also meant I had to be careful what I wrote about people - which is no bad thing – because they knew where to get me.

I would read what I had written back to my subjects when I was writing the Pendennis diary on the Observer. This meant that not only was I never stupidly cruel about people but also that I was also absolutely accurate in everything I wrote since these people were always invited to correct any inaccuracies. They then never had any awkward comeback. "Well I read it all back to you," I could say, "and you had your chance to correct it all then."

The problem with blogs is that there are no real figures or feedback in them so, quite early in our journey, Liz began posting my offerings on Facebook, easy enough when you have written the blog anyway since all you have to do is copy and paste it onto your Facebook page.

The only real difference with Facebook is that you can pay for a promotion which gets it around the Facebook manor. You can, of course, opt to pay nothing at all but, if you do that, the system simply doesn't work and you might end up with a response in low double figures. You can also direct the traffic to the country of your choice with a promotion, in my case Australia. I put a big promotion of more than £200 on one of my final posts on the so-called siege of Sydney and that got me almost everywhere in the land.

So I had been quietly Facebooking away when I posted what you have just read: The Crumbling Music of the Breaking Heart of God which, for me, clocked up an amazing 128,266 visits - on a promotion of £61 – with 1,187 likes and 61 shares. To get one "share" is difficult and rare because it means that the reader has gone to the trouble of posting it to all his friends. But to get 61 shares – with one alone going to perhaps a few hundred people with many of them posting it onwards - was almost beyond belief.

But why had the Aussies responded to that post in such numbers? Well, the headline about God's breaking heart is very eye-catching it is true but I also wrote sympathetically about the Aborigines and even suggested that they and the Aussies should both be stopped from drinking before it is too late. As a suggestion I thought that would go down like a cup of cold sick here in Australia but that wasn't the case at all and neither, from all the comments on my page, were my words about the Old Testament ways of God.

But the Aussies weren't supposed to believe in anything that they couldn't eat or drink. They weren't even supposed to understand a sentence unless it had three 'f' words in it.

So this was a real revelation about the Aussie psyche, I thought. Despite popular myth many of them clearly cared about the Aborigines and what happened to them. They didn't seem to mind at all my suggested ban on alcohol for all AND they were open to the mind and thoughts of God.

I was excited by these revelations and became even more excited by the thought that this book could become a sort of metaphysical detective story in which I would rummage through the roads of Australia, talking to people and getting a reaction to my findings from the public at large who would also react to me. I didn't have to read other books or stupid newspapers to find out who Australians were. I could get the whole picture for myself; what they thought and worried about and what made them get up in the morning. Then they could weigh in with their own views.

So this will become a real book, I am sure, written by someone who was beaten up by God as a teacher in Malaysia and given a new mandate on which he was left to work. He was indeed looked after while he worked on this mandate but couldn't finish the job because he felt he didn't have the right tools to finish it. Whatever those tools might be.

But now he had finally been given them and, as he travelled through the Bush, he'd surely become a fully-fledged prophet in his own right, not only explaining the wild words of God but echoing the thoughts and mind of the people too.

And what is more he wasn't any old prophet either, rampaging around the Bush, eating locusts and wild honey, dressed in sandals and a ragged gown but a thoroughly modern prophet in a winnebago, dongle in one hand and laptop in the other. Ah, how brighter might the Baptist's life have been if he'd had all that.

18: A Modern Noah

It is early on yet another sunlit morning in the coastal town of Broome in North West Australia and I am sitting in a caravan park near another prize jewel of a beach. Many of my fellow nomads have turned up over the past week or so but we have found plenty of space in the caravan parks since they are all far from booked up.

Many have described Broome as paradise but I can't wait to get away. At fifty dollars a night the sites are expensive compared to what we are used to and the other day a shop tried to charge me six dollars for a muffin. A muffin! The town itself, with all its new buildings and posh hotels, is well beyond the means of your average nomad and the sea is teeming with all kinds of stuff you simply would not want to bump into while out for a swim. In five minutes on one jetty we spotted a turtle, a jellyfish and large black and white sea snake which, we were told, was extremely poisonous. I enjoy swimming in the sea but certainly not with that kind of company.

The town itself would surely inspire a pretty good novel. The headquarters of the fire brigade once burned down, destroying the fire engine parked inside it. And, on the one and only time the bank was robbed, the robbers made their escapes on wobbling bicycles.

Just lately I had been busy sniffing around an extremely interesting story here which I have always wondered about, that of Lord McAlpine, former right hand man of Margaret Thatcher when she was in her pomp, and who died recently in his bed and breakfast in southern Italy, at the age of 71, unofficially of a broken heart. In all essentials it is the story of a man who accomplished a lot but never counted the cost.

This man whose building company, so the joke goes, put up the pyramids, was extremely rich and he tried to build a paradise on earth here in Broome. But the cost was too much even for his deep pockets and, when he was down, he was hit by scandalous and untrue allegations of child molestation from which he never really recovered. He was already in poor health but, according to his family, these allegations saw him off.

Actually his first purchase here in Broome was this Cable Beach complex where we are now parked up. He once owned 85 properties in Broome, including a brewery and McAlpine House, where he lived when he was in town. This house is a magnificent structure complete with latticework verandas and aviaries in the garden, one of which housed exotic birds including his prized collection of eclectus parrots. The house is now an expensive hotel even by Broome's expensive standards.

He also acquired – even though he didn't know it at the time since it came as part of a package - the quirky Sun Pictures, the world's oldest open-air picture garden where your enjoyment of such classics as Gone With The Wind might be considerably enhanced when you sat on their deckchairs as the mozzies, who bred in the grass in front of the screen, bit chunks out of your legs. Planes taking off from the nearby airport also appeared on the screens and, on high tides, which came no higher anywhere in the land than here, the sea would flood over the grass and you could find your feet drowning in its snake-infested waters as you ate your popcorn. That cinema is still there.

But it was for his zoo that McAlpine will always be remembered and one story had it that he bought the land for

A\$34m including the nearby beach and, to complete the deal, he signed a beer coaster in the Roebuck Bay Hotel. He also acquired dozens of rare Aboriginal artefacts and lots of master works of art including work by the great Sydney Nolan.

He started the zoo by collecting varieties of parrot, wild donkey, camels and buffalo. The 65 acres kept expanding with spacious paddocks for the antelope which bred well in them. He also collected nearly all the Australian species of parrot and built a ten-acre lake where wild birds prospered. Indeed his zoo was such a hit the local wild kangaroos were constantly trying to break in. He also, for the first time, bred a tiny fig parrot as well as pygmy hippos, started a cheetah breeding programme and managed to turn a burned-out 150 acres into a jungle amok with orchids.

But his schemes often did not sit well with the town which fought almost his every move with demonstrations and protests to the authorities. He was not embittered by this street fury, accepting it as the cost of democracy, but was soon in deep financial trouble. With the zoo in particular he had not factored in the enormous costs of specialised food for each animal. He also had to import experts, who are never cheap, and discovered he couldn't get close to covering his zoo costs with entry fees. A pilots' strike stopped visitors coming for a whole season and finally, this man, who always walked with the great and the good, saw his castles tumbling and had to sell off his assets.

Yet he is fondly remembered in Broome to this day, with his own statue on Cable Beach complete with parrot on his shoulder. He injected some A\$500m into the town and the population has gone from 4,800 when he first got here, to 15,000 today. Visitor numbers have gone up from 35,000 in 1983 to 237,000 now. Broome also boasts two strings of camels which carry tourists along the beach. The beasts fart happily with every step and those melodic farts are a pure joy to hear in the sunset.

Despite all this, I am fearful for this boomtown in the sun and am particularly afraid that, as happened to Lord McAlpine, all this growth is based on a quicksand of competing troubles which could make it sink as fast as it rose. After five days here we really wanted to get back on the road and out of it. The place has just become too expensive and there was another big problem festering away.

Yesterday Liz and I spent an afternoon in a park overlooking the sea near the main town caravan park. I got chatting to a young Dutch lad and he told me that a bloody fight had broken out amongst some twenty drunken Aborigines the night before in the Pioneers' Cemetery right next to us. Those buried there were all leading lights in the town's history including master pearlers who once did so much to contribute to the town's original wealth from pearl fishing. So what the fighting Aborigines had done was a bit like urinating on the holy altar and there was a lot of local fury about it all.

"It was unbelievable and extremely bloody fight and they kept sending their children into battle," the Dutch lad said. "When they weren't fighting amongst themselves they tried to terrorise us visitors and one man was sitting in front of his camper van drinking tea when he had his windscreen smashed. People down south just don't know what's going on. They haven't a clue what's happening here."

When people do find out what's going on here I believe that will kill the town's tourist business stone dead. People simply will not holiday here with their children if they feel unsafe or menaced by drunken idiots.

I say again that all Aborigines must all be stopped from drinking grog if they – or us – are going to have any chance at all of a decent, prosperous life here and indeed anywhere else in

Australia and judging by the 125,000 who visited my last post on this subject, there are a lot out there who agree with me.

All the towns that have stopped Aborigines from drinking alcohol have seen a marked decrease in violence, crime and domestic disputes. But the whites must also be stopped drinking. There should be a nationwide ban for all. You cannot stop some people from drinking and keep drinking yourselves. You simply cannot do it and I would say that the whole of Australia will stumble and fall unless a nationwide ban on alcohol is imposed on all.

I do not see that happening but ask how many bloody riots we need to see in these streets and how many young Aborigine kids do we need to see dangling from their schoolroom rafters before something is done.

***

I know all about the grog, certainly more than the hand-wringing liberals in the Canberra parliament since, as I have already said, I spent two long and painful years sitting nightly in a room with Alcoholics Anonymous. Even so I could not fully explain the carnage alcohol wreaks, on an almost hourly basis, on your health, wealth, marriages and sanity. As soon as you pick up one drink you become half the man you were.

Even church missionaries gave up on Aborigines when they were allowed to drink again. They knew there was nothing they could do with drunks. Also remember my artist friend, Mark Norval of Derby, who saw fifty of his pupils kill themselves because of their drunken, abusive parents and Mark even tried to kill himself after cutting down one too many.

Think of this carefully Australia since like Lord McAlpine, who never counted the cost of anything, you are very close to throwing it all away because you really do know the cost but are ignoring it. You have one chance and one chance only and that lies in you all embracing the miracle of recovery and sobriety.

Yet it was here I first began nursing another suspicion when I learned that there had never been a study of the effect of television on the Aboriginal communities. Oh hadn't there? I could just see them sitting in their tribal home around a television showing Breaking Bad or True Detective and the fighting in the Pioneer's Cemetery began making an awful lot of sense.

But, as ever, it is always the question of proving the link which hangs over writers like me. Whenever the creators of violent and films are attacked their response is always the same. Where's the proof? Well there's plenty of proof, plenty of academic research making the connection but such research is always ignored largely because it is often so very difficult to list and explain in, say, a studio situation when confronted with a nutty maker of violent films.

I have often thought that simple reportage could easily, if not entertainingly, establish the link and remember one brilliant piece of reportage by Brian Keenan in his wonderful book about his hostage years in Beirut, An Evil Cradling. He tellingly describes the impact of a Rambo film on an uneducated and unsophisticated audience there and I would say his description tells us more than a hundred bodies of research on the subject. This is a masterful report which, like the rest of the book, is full of truth and insight and I only wish someone would send Keenan into the Australian Bush to stay with the Aborigines and report on what he found.

"This man (Rambo), unresolved in himself, chooses to take up arms against his sea of troubles. He carries his Kalashnikov on his arm, his handgun stuck in the waistband of his trousers, a belt of bullets slung around his shoulders. I had seen so many in Beirut thus attired. Their weapons hanging from them and glistening in the sun. The guns were symbols of potency. The men were dressed as caricatures of Rambo. Many of them wore a headband tied and knotted at the side above the ear, just as the character in the movie had done. It is a curious paradox that this Rambo figure, this all-American hero, was the stereotype these young revolutionaries had adopted. They had taken on the cult figure of the Great Satan they had so despised and who they claimed was responsible for all the evil in the world. Emulating Rambo they would reconquer the world and simultaneously rid themselves of that inadequacy they would never admit.

"We sat there in the darkened cinema," Keegan continues, "and, as each character pulled out his weapon and began firing furiously, the young Arab men around us would moan and groan in a kind of ecstasy, crying out the names of the weapons. All around us in the cinema you could hear the words 'Kalashnikov, Kalashnikov. Beretta, Beretta'. These young men knew the names of every type of gun, even the names of the mortars and rocket-launchers. The cinema rang with the chant of excited worship."

19: How Neil the Nomad dug up a Crock of Gold

We have been mooching down the west coast but not hurrying in any way, hoping to get to Perth at the start of Spring when, we are told, everything erupts into dazzling displays of flowers and new life.

Meanwhile we stop on beaches and caravan sites whose facilities are so lousy everyone in a prisoner of war camp would go on strike if they had to put up with them. There is often no roof on the shower units with corrugated iron doors hanging sideways. Rusty nails serve as coat hangers and scrawled notices tell you to put the lid down on the toilets to keep out the frogs. As you sit there worrying about frogs a giant centipede might wander past your feet doubtless on his way to somewhere nice. At least such places are cheap.

Yet everyone remains relentlessly cheerful even if the pans are full of frogs and the floors are amok with centipedes. The nomads all gather for happy hour as usual late in the afternoon and they're all in bed by nine o'clock at the latest. On our last site a group of youngsters began making a lot of noise after nine o'clock – some of them even singing! - and were all threatened with immediate eviction.

I am writing this in Barn Hill Station, perched amongst many trees on the edge of red sand cliffs guarding a foaming Indian Ocean, wondering what to write about when my attention is caught by Neil, who is watering a patch of plants just outside his rig which, he tells me, he grew from seedlings when he first got here.

He's got just about everything on his small plot: mustard, radish, rocket, tomatoes (four different types) parsley, butter beans and climbing beans. His crops are only ever menaced by the station's chickens, he says, and if ever they are caught at it, they are for sure all going to end up in a chicken stew.

I found Neil's story about his vegetables interesting, showing how even the nomads need to develop a relationship with the land, no matter how short their stays and, when I went back to him to check on his list, I asked him what he was going to do next and he told me that he and his wife Loretta were both going to go gold prospecting in Kalgoorlie. Oh were they really? Did they manage to find any?

You bet. Last year they dug up gold worth A$60,000 in three weeks. He didn't plan to sell it or anything like that but hoped to leave each of his children a huge glass case full of mounted gold nuggets. He was going to have to dig up a fair bit more, it would appear, since they had five children aged between 40 and 47 and so far he'd only got enough to fill three cases.

But you can't just grab a shovel and head out into the Bush and start digging holes, it turned out, since, in the Australian way, they have a ton of rules even for the Bush and you have to go through myriad hoops to get the necessary permissions, beginning with the Department of Petroleum and Minerals in Perth where you get a Miner's Right for A$25. Then you are advised to join the Australian Prospectors and Leaseholders' Association for A$60 a year which will insure you in the event of injury while digging your holes.

Next you must log on to a website, Tengraph, which covers all Australian mining areas, to find where you may or may not dig and for how long. There are plenty of gold police working throughout the Bush who will make sure you stick to what you have registered for and the fine can be A$100,000, plus the loss of your rig, if you are caught stealing gold. Many have been done like this.

Neil added that you soon get to know where the land has been worked because there will be lots of scratch marks left by previous prospectors and that's a good place to start digging because, if successful, they never go deep enough and hurry home more than happy with what they have already dug up.

His lovely wife often works on old areas like this, which have yielded gold, and she has usually done better than Neil although, he says, there is never any sense of competition between them. Lots of people do better than him, he says, but he did know one man who had never had any luck in six years of tunnelling. Another didn't have a good deal of luck either until he discovered he was wearing steel-capped shoes which kept playing up his metal detector.

Luck does indeed play a big part but you do need to study the land too. Under a big bush is a good place to start or a tree trunk that's been lying there for years. But you've also got to be careful with techniques and settings on your metal detector. Neil has a top-line detector worth A$8,000 with 200 settings and you also have to understand the weather to get your settings right. A threatening storm might mean you have to change everything.

You can sell your gold at the Perth Mint who will charge 10 per cent plus the cost of the assay. Otherwise you can sell it through magazines and there is a steady market for it. The world still loves gold.

Liz and I might try it and we might not. I find it difficult enough breathing in this heat let alone wandering around the Bush with a huge shovel and digging holes in the ground in the obviously doomed hope of finding a lump of gold at the bottom of them. Also, to be perfectly honest, I could never do the paperwork and I'm not even sure Liz could either, even if she wanted to.

20: Cyclones, Fires and Locusts as the Language of God

Another day, another campsite. We have been cruising south down these wonderful Australian roads and then we might have to take a turn-off and it could be a 10-mile stretch of washboard road, all rattling bumps and teeth-shaking furrows, before we drive into another strange place on the sea full of odd people, some with parrots who swear and others with dogs that whine. Travellers like to take their pets with them although dogs are banned in some places, like the national parks.

Today we are in Eighty Mile Beach, a few hundred of us camped on a curving foreshore, lined by palms and where you can just sit back and listen to the lazy whoosh of the waves on the huge stretch of sand, some eighty miles of it would you believe. This is a good moment for prayer too: just face the sun and close your eyes and you might even be amazed where this prayer will take you as a celestial blaze fills your brain.

Yet enjoyment of such places can often be determined by your neighbours or, more specifically, your neighbours' noise and you are not encouraged to move, once placed, even if you find that noise distressing. Here we have a family of four in a tent next to us and I'm finding them very distressing indeed.

The mother likes to listen to Chinese music very loudly on her radio and spends many hours talking loudly in Chinese, possibly to her gossip-starved mother in downtown Shanghai. As she's listening to her mother, with the aid of a giant earpiece, her children keep shouting to her and are always ignored. The boy has asked her, maybe twenty times that morning, if they can light a fire but never gets a yes or a no. Father is off with his metal detector on the beach and, when he returns, hasn't much to say to his children either, presumably sulking because he hasn't managed to detect anything worth having. It's an example of a family who, like so many other dysfunctional families everywhere, cannot speak to – or listen to – one another.

Yes, noise has a lot to answer for but I was interested to learn that, here on Eighty Mile Beach, it could have been far worse. One regular couple with a huge rig used to turn up here every summer and they even carried their own kitchen garden in a trailer. In their lounge they had a large Versailles-type chandelier and a real organ. At certain times day or night the wife would take out a bottle of fine wine and sit in her armchair under her chandelier on full glint and that was the cue for the husband to set up his organ and serenade her as she glugged her wine. Some may have enjoyed such a concert but I must say I would have gone absolutely berserk had said organist begun blasting away the Hallelujah Chorus in the middle of the night particularly if his drunken missus was snoring away, legs splayed apart on her armchair, having finished one, if not several bottles, of her fine wine.

Later that night we were both trying to sleep but our Chinese neighbour had clearly thought of something else to tell her mother in Shanghai. This went on at great length and I cracked, begging Liz to ignore the camp rules and get up to drive us somewhere, anywhere, away from this Chinese hell. Liz wasn't at all happy with this because there is a lot to put away and unplug, including electricity, water and waste, before you can drive this thing anywhere. But I promised her a bottle of fine wine for her troubles - I had stashed one away behind the bath - and that seemed to do the trick. She still likes the odd drink even if I don't.

Half an hour later we drove off into the night furtively like a couple doing a midnight flit owing the landlord six months' rent. We ended up in the middle of an empty field next to the shore where, nourished by plenty of silence except for the watery sighs of small waves, we immediately settled back down into a heaven and slept the sleep of the dead. Even the chattering palm fronds sent out hints of paradise at dawn as pairs of huge butterflies appeared over the neighbouring sand dunes, tumbling around one another, as they fluttered past us.

It is truly extraordinary what you see just sitting outside rigs like ours nursing a cup of tea watching the daybreak here in Oz. A kookaburra landed on the table in front of me, spotted a fat dragonfly which he immediately scoffed and flew away again. A large black ibis next wandered past with his long curving beak pecking at the earth looking for whatever it is that black ibises like to eat. Way over the sand dunes the whole beach was another stunning revelation of morning beauty.

The shop sold a guide to the 28-odd different shells you can find in abundance on the beach – everything from trumpet shells to gastropods – and, on each rising tide, whole rows of anglers were out there pulling in fish I have never seen before let alone heard of. The women seemed particularly good at this while many of the men sat on chairs watching, sometimes stirring themselves if the fish looked a big 'un which might require a muscular touch.

***

Yes, this is paradise on earth all right but, as we all know, even paradise can come at a high cost; it can all be blown away again within minutes, as it was when a cyclonic tide swamped this place in the early eighties, destroying the site and everything on it. It was rebuilt and destroyed again in 1994 by Cyclone Annette with wind speeds of 228km an hour, smashing up the beach huts, tearing down the trees and leaving many of them uprooted and dead where they lie in black tangled heaps at the entrance to this site even to this day. In 2009 Cyclone Laurence came charging through here at speeds of 289km an hour and the destruction was so complete the owners didn't know where to start re-building.

Then, in a variation of the old curses, a swarm of locusts hit the place destroying all the site's lawns in one hour flat.

I spoke to one young man in the coffee lounge here, a baker who was travelling to Broome looking for work. You might be travelling along when a locust would hit your car and then another and another, he told me. Within an hour the sun will seem to have turned completely black as you are engulfed by locusts which will get into your engine and every corner of your rig and even your pyjamas. They will eat everything and, after they have left, will leave eggs which will hatch in a few weeks and the whole cycle will repeat itself with another black, hungry swarm swirling around in the sunshine wondering what to scoff next.

Forest fires are a perpetual danger, he went on, and there is only one thing to do with these fires and that is flee them. Some do try staying in their homes, perhaps sitting in a bath of cold water, but they almost always perish.

***

As I have written before I find something completely absorbing about these dark explosions of the natural world. They talk to me of a living God and his penchant for great outbursts of anger, of his language and turbulence and readiness to show his sensitivity. You can see what happened when he got upset throughout the Old Testament, sending an angel to destroy the Assyrian army and even turning a woman into a block of salt, actions he later regretted.

Throughout the New Testament he calms down a lot, pleased with his son who became a living beacon of love. But current events suggest he is ill at ease again and might be getting back to his Old Testament ways, angry with a people who have largely turned their back on him, particularly the white Australians and the way they are destroying the Aborigines by feeding them with deadly poisons of grog.

When God is being openly and deliberately thwarted we should at least understand that things can go wrong in the space of a very short minute. We should never get complacent. I love God but am deeply afraid of him too and worry what he might do the way things are going. As I have written before he beat me practically senseless one dark night in Malaysia when he saw how people like me – as I was then – were doing to his world. Even fifty years later I still haven't recovered from that beating, still suffer from headaches for days on end. I very badly don't want it to happen again and the reason I drank so much for so many years was to calm down those headaches which often accompanied a thickening anxiety. Drink seemed to be the only medicine that worked and God never bothered me when I was drunk. Now I just put up with the headaches which still settle on me whenever I get anxious about something, particularly something to do with him.

Cyclones and hurricanes and locusts can also be seen as symptoms of God's own anxiety, I would suggest and, given that he can have a short fuse it could also mean that it might be the fire next time.

God gave Noah the rainbow sign, no more water but the fire next time.

∗∗∗

My notion that is possible and even desirable to write a book in close partnership with the people you are writing about; that I might even be able to start a dialogue between the people of Australia and Wales seems to have legs. While I am not yet at all sure where my postings on Facebook will take me I've already discovered another great advantage in it since, if the post doesn't work for the reader, he will tell you and you can chop it which, overall, I'm sure, should improve the work no end.

I have already canned three posts for not coming up to snuff in the eyes of my readers and you can't help but wonder if many other books would have been improved if other authors did the same. My readers are also never slow in telling me if they think my piece is too long, too daft or too crude.

At this stage in the journey I had written a post – Old Age Is Not for Cissies – in which I ruminated on the health and activities of the Grey Nomads who often struggled on the campsites forever forgetting what they were supposed to be doing. I described how some of them might go to the toilet block in the middle of the night and forget why they had gone there in the first place or couldn't get in because they had forgotten their glasses and couldn't key in the code to open the door.

I must say I didn't think much of the piece when I wrote it – full of cheap shots at the old - in which I include myself - and neither did my readers since it got a mere 324 visits and just one measly share. Two of my closest friends had also objected to it quite strenuously.

All authors write stuff which they are not sure about but throw it into the mix anyway but I now felt I had no alternative but to can the pieces which no one much liked including, on reflection, the author. It's very revealing and even interesting that Facebookers appear to know what they like. They show up in droves when they sense the post might be something they really go for and all but go missing when they don't.

This net is a truly wonderful creation, as all terrorists seem to have worked out for themselves. ISIS works the net remorselessly which tells me the good guys should also get in there and do the same.

My last post, which you have just read - Cyclones, Fires and Locusts as the Language of God - clocked up an impressive 106,808 visits with 1,187 likes on a promotion of £130. This had clearly gone down as sweet as a nut with my growing mob even though I had been writing about God in it, a subject which many seem to want to avoid these days. Yet these figures told me there were plenty of people who really approved of my writing about God and I was free to go in a direction I had earlier been afraid of.

I've said before I was puzzled as to what tone I should take in this book but these figures clearly told me that my readers didn't mind some comedy but seriousness was welcome too. I could indeed dive deep and, if I were then so moved, go deeper and I might well carry my readers with me. Such things are useful to know when you are writing a book. They stop you feeling the need to pick up a drink too, which is why most writers probably drink so much.

So I wasn't going to end up a lonely preacher in a damp chapel pounding the pulpit before half a dozen old ladies and a couple of cabbages. Yet I might even now be presiding over a huge electronic church in which I had begun addressing congregations of more than 106,000, which would keep growing exponentially to what? Well that would clearly very much depend on what I wrote and if what I wrote actually chimed with my readers' minds and thoughts.

But I would continue with some comedy of course and my next offering – a satire on the horrible town of Port Hedland - brought me a decent 29,840 visits with 52 likes on a promotion of £59. I was perfectly happy with that but couldn't even start guessing at the size of the uproar to come when my 106,808 was going to more than double. God knew perfectly well what was to come of course and I did wonder if he was laughing about it already.

21: Port Hedland Voted Worst Town in Oz Ever

Port Hedland has just won the national prize for the worst town in Oz, I can exclusively reveal. There was a lot of stiff competition for this coveted prize but, after a long debate, the judges decided to make this award stand forever. No matter how hard they debated the judges just couldn't see any real competition for this award coming from any other quarter. About the only positive thing they could say about the place was that it looked good in the dark.

The approach to the town was one of its most striking features, their report noted. You get whole swathes of mud and salt flats – 6,000 hectares in all - where Rio Tinto dries out the seawater and builds giant white castles of salt which gives the place a strong horror B-film atmosphere.

The land surrounding the town looks pretty B-film too, full of road trains piled with iron ore storming up and down the streets all looking as if they are in Le Mans. You keep waiting for them to overtake one another until you realise they are all joined together. Even larger than the road trains are the real trains with their wagons, some of them 5km long which rumble over the townscape continuously like endless hangovers.

Then as you enter the town looking for real castles and town halls you come across active smelters and gas processing plants leaking their industrial smoke everywhere. It's easy enough to park in the streets though - even for a rig of our size - since no one else seems to want to park there. The houses and rooftops are all made of the same corrugated iron, ensuring they are, hopefully, cyclone-proof in this the most cyclone-visited town in Australia. Everywhere there are warnings of what to do – or where to take shelter - if a cyclone hits.

Iron ore has made Port Hedland one of the richest towns in Australia. Some thirty ships anchor offshore each day waiting for their turn to come in and load up with the ore before travelling back to China or Japan. Recently they managed to service eight ships on one tide. Each ship pays A$100,000 a day for the pleasure of waiting out at anchor. It's far cheaper to wait than to go away and come back to try again – and many are forced to wait up to ten days for their turn. Do the math.

But except for a few small parks – one with a musical public lavatory – very little has been spent on culture of any sort. The museum is as cold and dull as a mother-in-law's kiss. You pay three dollars a head to go into the two small corrugated sheds where you can look at a few immediately forgettable dusty items, all guarded by a curator who seems to have far more important things to do except talk to visitors and explain why this museum, in one of the richest towns in Australia, is so completely useless and in urgent need of a good cyclone to take it away before starting again.

There is an art gallery – oh yes – with just one interesting living exhibit in the form of a yellow and green frog dwelling in total luxury just inside the lip of the toilet pan. This frog in the bog just looks up at you and even seems to beam up at you happily as you flush. He's probably one of the few inhabitants of Hedland who is completely happy with his rent-free home and, when asked if perhaps they should evict him, the lady in charge of the gallery just laughed. "He's not doing no harm."

The tour of the harbour – at a hefty forty five dollars a head – is little more than an hour long poodle on a small launch around the water looking up at dull oil tankers from which, if you are lucky, one of the crew will wave back at you. The real purpose of the launch is to take visiting sailors ashore to have a few drinks perhaps or do some shopping. Visitors have clearly been appended to these tours to make money out of an already existing service. The sailors are always, quite rightly, first off and on.

One sailor visiting Hedland bought a new camera recently but got so carried away with his new acquisition the police caught him trying to take a shot up a woman's skirt on the store stairs. Oddly enough two of the news clippings recording this sad event are pinned to the notice board in the Seaman's Mission. Our judges found it extraordinary that the Mission seemed proud of this. Why didn't they make him a Freeman of the town and be done with it?

Also best avoided, if possible, are the motor repair garages, manned by FIFOs (Fly In Fly Outs) who fly in from places as far as Perth for three weeks before flying home for a week off. These men are paid well and charge accordingly, becoming sharks ceaselessly patrolling the muddied waters of mechanical failure, often taking huge bites out of visitors' pocket books. They like to tow you back into their repair shops – often under any pretext like a leak or a blown fuse - and their mileage rates are phenomenal.

One man was told last week that it would cost him A$2,300 to get towed 20km into Hedland and he only had a water leak from a loose hosepipe which, after looking a bit more closely at the engine, he managed to fix himself.

The campsite at Cooke Point, with a nice view of the glittering lights of industrial Hedland when the sun goes down, earned a few favourable comments from the panel although that was ruined when it was reported a large and possibly starving crocodile had been seen running around in a dried-up creek just below the main camping area. Well at least the children's play area had been fenced off with iron bars which not even a starving crocodile could get through, the panel were told, but they unanimously decided Hedland had worked really hard to win the main prize. And keep it for good.

At the time of writing nothing had been resolved and it is understood that Hedland has, in fact, flatly refused to accept its prize although the council remains anxious to accept the substantial cash award that goes with it. The council has been told that this is impossible. No acceptance, no cash. But it is also understood that, even at this late stage, the council is actually reviewing its position and will possibly use the prize to paint all the houses there in primary colours which might brighten up the place no end and, there again, might not.

22: Songs in Praise of this Raw Red Earth

I just about managed to avoid drinking myself to death some thirty years ago when I left journalism to become a full-time writer but it was a close-run thing.

Since then I have produced eighteen books and it hasn't been easy – certainly not profitable. Yet every time I sat down as a writer, at about 10.30 in the morning, there was always a sliver of ice buried deep in my insides since, without fail, I was convinced that this morning everything would come to an end and that this was the day the tide fully went out never to return. I would not be able to string together a single sentence let alone write one down.

I am saying this because a sense of easy creativity has enveloped me here in Australia. My pen doesn't pause a moment and I'm up and running. There is always something new and exciting to write about in a land which is always so generous with herself and I often wish I had found Australia ten or twenty years ago since, had I been allowed to come and live here, I would certainly have become a writer of the Bush, telling the stories of these wonderful people, all set in their extraordinary landscape.

I would also have attempted to tell the Aussies what's on God's mind. They don't get much of that out here – maybe not any - but, whether they know it or not, that's exactly what they need to learn about at a time when God has fully submitted himself to a struggle with a great tide of evil which is flooding the world with increasing violence; a struggle, what is more, which he is not bound to win.

This is, I believe, the only real story of our times and why I keep trying to write it.

Perhaps predictably the Welsh have pretty much ignored my attempts to explain the secrets of God's mind to them. Many think I am mad but what do they know? Wales has always been a religious country and our very soul was hammered out by the preacher in his battered pulpit; our story has been a long one of creative preachers who could jerk people out of their conventional mood with the thunder and lightning of their oratory. But not any more they don't. Judging by our emptying churches and chapels most of the three million Welsh are spiritually dead without so much as a snowballs' chance in hell of ever coming alive in the spirit again.

But what a brilliant setting for another religious revival Australia would make. This is a land full of passion and shooting stars. A revival here would bring us closer to God and make the very landscape sing with new things. Oh yes, this country is absolutely perfect for another lightning strike of the Holy Spirit.

***

Three days ago we drove out of Point Samson after staying a week there and, at the site exit, we passed a giant wheelie bin with about twenty sulphur-crested cockatoos all screeching and fighting one another over the rubbish piled up in it. We'd had a real blast in Samson, attending a local race meeting where we lost a little and where many of the local girls, dressed in their finery, ended up flat on their backs after winning too much money on the horses and hitting the grog too hard. It really isn't just the Aborigines that the grog doesn't agree with.

We also watched a golden moon dip over the horizon, leaving amazing shimmering stepping stones on the sea, and visited the ruined town of Cossack, where pearling had first started in Australia, looking around the old cemetery there and discovering that pearling was clearly not good for your health or longevity since barely anyone laid to rest there ever lived much over the age of forty.

A few minutes after leaving Samson we pulled in to fill up with diesel and on the way out of the petrol station braked to watch a dingo walking down the road followed by a pup. A dingo! The legendary Australian wild dog, who has been in this country for 3,000 years, just trotting along there, casting an anxious look back at her youngster making sure he was keeping up. The fleabag wasn't slightly concerned about us watching her either and I'm told there are now more of them than ever, more successful than even the crocodiles as they scavenge the towns and Bush for food, even raping any poor domestic dogs they might catch wandering about the streets on their own late at night.

We weren't too sure where we were going to drive next since the latest weather report had told us that cyclones were tearing apart the suburbs of Perth, where we were aiming for, and a forest fire was threatening Broome from where we had just escaped. Chased by forest fires and threatened by cyclones while passing mad cockatoos and wandering dingoes. How could any writer fail to be inspired by an opening like that?

But, in truth, I didn't think I had the wherewithal at my age to tackle another novel which can take a minimum of at least two or three years' hard work. Then the publisher might well give it a dodgy cover, in your least favourite colour and, what is more, try his best to keep the publication a top secret. All in all being a writer was never a barrel of laughs or money.

So we headed for Exmouth and those huge termite mounds were back with us again when lo, we also saw sheep for the first time this trip, out there among their new lambs, always a sign back home in Wales that spring is about to burst. Those lambs don't seem to mind having to start their lives in the Welsh mountain winter, the freezing farmers going out in the middle of the night to dig them out of snow drifts or pulling them out of the unyielding backsides of their unhappy mothers.

But Australian sheep always seem to have warm sunshine to greet them which must amount to as good a start as any. What they eat here though is a mystery; it's certainly not grass because there ain't any.

And then, absolutely out of nowhere, two suicidal emus ran out on to the road in front of us. They just about made it safely after a bit of swerving by Liz, but then a third came crashing out of the Bush after them and it looked a dead cert that we would run him over, making a terrible mess of our rig and an even bigger mess of him. Locals call these emus powder puffs because they explode on impact. I screamed at Liz to brake but, wise girl, she took no notice of me and just slowed down a bit, miraculously managing to find a path between them.

This encounter gave Liz goosebumps and we had to stop for a calming cup of tea. Australia! You think you might be getting a bit bored and the next thing you are nearly murdering a full-grown emu and in dire need of a cup of tea - which I even managed to make.

***

My thoughts about how I might have become a writer of the Bush had been prompted by an encounter with an Irishman who gloried in the name of Outback Paddy, aka Michael Blake, a wiry youngster of 66, as lean as a butcher's bike and with a head as bald as a billiard ball.

Outback Paddy – a fellow Celt – is not a writer as such but a talented musician and singer who travels around Western Australia entertaining anyone who will listen to his songs which are almost always full of praise for the many faces of his adopted homeland. He describes himself as a Grey Nomad who, in his turn, has become the Voice of the Grey Nomads.

He has now fully turned his back on his native Ireland and calls Australia home, wandering the country in his caravan, singing songs of praise about things like the moonbeams of Broome, the long, lonely ride across the great Nullarbor Plain and the horses and waterfalls of his home town in the Kimberleys.

They are all lovely, clear songs about this enthralling country, sung in a fine tenor which Liz thinks has a lot of sadness in it. If he was actually sad he didn't tell me much about it although he did lose his wife in a car crash two years after getting here in 1986 and that must still hurt a lot.

But how deeply satisfying it must be to wander this holy land singing the praises of a country he loves so much. In the old days in Wales he would have been known as a wandering Praise Poet, giving God and his whole creation the praise he so loves to hear. His funniest and sweetest lines however are about the Grey Nomads of whom he is a proud member.

"Those grey-haired granddads who do it just for me, happy to be retired and free. Taking their suppers by a creek or river bed under a Halloween moon and shooting stars, way up over head."

His definition of a Grey Nomad is one who has no home and lives solely in his rig. Such full-timers probably number around 30,000 who are out and about in all weathers, he said, and will keep driving around until the end. I liked Paddy and felt close to him, the both of us now out on the roads of Oz doing what we both love. He, of course, found his subject early enough and, arguably, I have found mine too late. But there's still time enough for both of us to pursue our couplets and visions, latter-day praise poets always wondering what the next bend will bring.

23: The Tremulous Love Song of the Lonely Aussie Whale

You don't normally think of love when you look at the sea – at least I don't – but this sunshine morning the very depths of the Indian Ocean are full of it, either singing songs of a broken heart in the fathomless deep or surfing in on the rolling seahorses with bouncing leaps of joy.

We are on the shoreline below the lighthouse in Ningaloo Marine Park, just outside Exmouth, the most westerly, hottest and driest part of Australia. More than 200 species of fish live on this reef including grouper, angelfish, barracuda and numerous turtles. But today we are focusing on the whales who, having given birth – or about to do so – are all swarming around in the waves in front of us in a sort of giant fantasy of squirts.

There are about fourteen of them, all squirting away, and occasionally, a whole mass of blubber comes exploding up from the depths, twisting its whole body in one great spasm of joy. He's just scored big-time; you can tell by his whooping behaviour. All the little squirts attest to that too and the families are all heading down below the Tropic of Capricorn to rest up before the next time.

It's not easy being a whale. You've got to do all kinds of things before getting to this position, the first of which, obviously, is to find a mate. Their way of doing this is extremely moving since they will sing love songs to one another and these songs are the most doleful of the seven seas; they positively ache with sorrow and loneliness. We might be listening to the great cries of the purest pain as if from a mother in the middle of a battlefield where all the soldiers have been slain. This really is a song once heard never forgotten.

Research suggests that such cries will also warn off other males who might be after their women or else might attract females who can judge them by how well they hold their songs together. Females can also work out how fit or hot a man might be from his song and there are males who do nothing but sing whenever they come close to females. So one way or another the whole whale scene is pretty musical.

When I was little with nothing else to do but wander the streets of Cardiff, my mind locked in endless daydreams, usually about girls, I liked to go to the National Museum and one morning went inside to discover they had a new exhibition on whales.

The impact of the sound I heard on entry was immediate, powerful and lasting; it was a long yodelling outpouring of beckoning and loss. "You are listening to the love song of the whale," a very Welsh voice, possibly that of a preacher, said. "He always sings like this when he is trying to find a new mate. These songs can be heard for miles in the whale waters of the world and, a far as we know, they always work."

Oh, I could do with one of them, I thought inanely after seeing the exhibition and saw myself wandering the streets of Wales, singing whale stuff into a megaphone. The young girls would hurry from everywhere in the land to find me: on trains and buses and their own two feet, unable to bear all this sorrow in their ears any longer, all wanting to fix me.

152

Well that plan didn't quite work out – rather like a lot of other dopey plans I hatched when I was young – and here we are now, more than sixty years later, sailing out in a small boat beyond the reef, with Ningaloo Ecology Cruises, trying to get near the whales who have been squirting their blowholes ragged around these parts for the past week or so. Except there seems to be one big problem insofar as, today at least, they all seem to have squirted off elsewhere.

Next comes an even bigger problem since I discover, to my complete horror, because no one had told me, that this trip was not to see whales at all but a snorkelling trip on which we are invited to dive on to the reef and swim with whatever we find down there. They were even laying on snorkels and masks. "Well I didn't know about any of this," I cry to Alek, the skipper. "I came on this trip to get a close look at whales and I haven't even brought my bathers."

"No probs," Alek replies in cheerful Aussie-speak. "You can go in with your underpants. The others won't mind, will you girls?" There are about five young girls on this trip, including one wearing a burka who, as it goes, doesn't seem slightly amused by what she might see.

Thus it was that I was togged up only in my ill-fitting boxer shorts, given a snorkel and a mask and flippers and pretty much thrown over the side with about eight others. When I hit the water I was too frightened and embarrassed to be cold but, as I thrashed around trying to get my breathing under control, I could never have known I was about to go through one of the great   if not greatest - moments of my life.

I had once tried scuba diving some thirty years ago in Montego Bay but had been thrown out of the sea for being useless.

So snorkel and mask were not new to me and I soon got on top of my breathing and even stopped worrying about what might end up hanging out of my underpants and, more to the point, whether some huge, hungry fish with lots of teeth might spot it.

But I quickly calmed down, turning one way and another before swimming straight into a brilliantly lit heaven and a swarm of about a hundred damsel neons, all bright purple with yellow tails who kept swimming around me, not even scarpering when I reached out to them. Next I came up against a huge yellow-striped angelfish who took one look at me and buzzed off fast.

At this point everything became ever more lovely with the sunshine lighting up the huge coral bommies as a whole range of fish and other beasties slid past me silently, including a yellow boxfish which really is shaped like a yellow box, now followed by a parrotfish who was so gaudily coloured he almost took away what little there was left of my breath.

There was also the silent music of the coral in the shape of the shrimps, anemones, clams and crabs – all skirting around one another in one long and incomprehensible celebration of survival. Next I was swimming close to a mind-boggling swarm of silver emperors and then, motionless just above the sand, were five barracuda all hanging out together doing nothing. Next to appear was a giant grouper, almost as big as me, lying there, half concealed by a rock, waiting for fish to go past which he duly sucked in. He was far too grand to chase after fish was this grouper, I learned later, just used his giant lungs to suck in his prey in as they finned their way past.

It was all like one glorious vision from which there was no awakening: a long ambition fully realised - and all in my boxers too. I knew, as soon as I surfaced, I would carry those golden moments, in full, in my mind and heart for the rest of my days.

24: "Count your toes before you go in and count 'em again when you come out."

After seeing the wonders under the sea at Ningaloo we continue wandering the Australian roads like lost breezes and I am keen to dive again – not in my boxers, but with the proper gear, venturing into deep, dark caves perhaps and facing up to whatever might be facing me. Interestingly and perhaps even significantly all the previous problems with my feet seem to have disappeared and every bit of me is fighting fit.

We have now got to Coral Bay, another incredible chunk of pure paradise built around a curving white sandy beach with palms leaning over a lagoon of the deepest blue. You can see the fish swimming around from the beach and every other day they feed these fish by hand and about fifty huge snappers flail around for tit-bits from the visitors. Yes, this is it. I am going to become a fully kitted-out diver who, in the week we are here, is going to become on first name terms with every fish in the lagoon.

I wandered out into the water and was standing there up to my waist when two Aussies joined me and we had a bit of a chat. In Oz a bit of a chat always means anything up to half an hour – and never any less – as we unpack the meaning of life, what their family has been doing lately or what's wrong with their rig.

As this chat proceeded I was about to take off for a swim when we spotted a quite sizeable stingray settled in the sand about three feet away. We looked some more and spotted three others surrounding us. They can move away from you very fast if they spot you coming in their direction, I now know, and while they won't kill you, they will give you a very nasty bang if you do happen to step on one.

I backed slowly out of the water and went to buy Liz an ice cream. I wasn't taking any chances. In Broome I'd met a man who'd had his finger bitten off by a shark. And he was supposedly safe in a cage at the time. Apparently he was giving one shark a good scratch through the bars of the cage when another swooped down out of nowhere and took off with his scratching finger.

The next day the same group gathered for a chat in the lagoon when we heard some bad news. A blowfish – or north west blowy – had just bitten off one of our fellow traveller's little toes on the very spot we'd spotted the stingrays and she had to be stretchered off by the flying doctor to hospital in Perth. They were concerned she might develop an infection and had been pumping her with drugs which made her throw up all night. But apart from her missing toe she was fine, or as fine as you might expect to be after a fish had made off with your little toe.

Next thing we learned that another of our number had been attacked by another starving blowy and she was fearful she was going to lose her two middle toes, yelling out: "He's got me, he's got me." But he hadn't got her and Val's toes were left bloodied but intact.

A young lad had a big hole bitten out of one of his swimming fins and was quite desolate that he might not be able to use them for snorkelling ever again.

These blowys are worse than piranhas, one of the nastiest creatures in the seven seas. They have saw teeth that can rip a horse apart when they are hungry - which is most of the time - and are very aggressive, ready to eat anything. One of the local rangers told me that he had actually seen a blowy chase a man out of the water and across the sand to try and drag him back into the sea before rolling over and dying himself. Quite mad too.

So I immediately gave up all thought of ever swimming here in Coral Bay and asked around amongst those working there about how many such attacks had happened. A lot of them suddenly developed a severe difficulty with the English language while Grant, the owner of the shellfish shop on the front, began throwing his hands around shouting: "I've been here twenty-six years and this is the first time I've ever seen anything like this. That fish is a one-off which just got into the bay here. It may never happen again ever."

I'm even thinking Grant looks like the mayor in Jaws who keeps telling everyone there's no Big White around since he might run amok and ruin the town's tourist trade. "It's nothing," Grant goes on. "Just a hiccup. No one's been really hurt."

It was my turn to get agitated and I'm thinking Grant should screw his head back on. "A woman has lost one of her toes and another nearly lost two," I shout. "How many toes do you need to lose around here before anyone takes these blowfish seriously?"

The park ranger does appear to be more concerned than Grant saying that he had been having discussions with the owner of the place about putting up warning signs on the beach. "We'll probably do it but we're not at all sure what good it might do. Anyone who swims here knows they are taking some kind of risk."

Anyway that's the end of my diving career for sure. I'm going back to being a real Grey Nomad on dusty roads and that's easier on the nerves all round.

25: After the Thorns a Gorgeous Crown of Wild Flowers

You stand by the side of the grey bitumen road in WA and look at the red earth swarming against it. You pick up a handful and let the red dust trickle through your fingers, much of it being shaken around in the slight breeze. You are completely surrounded by the endless Bush where huge red stones are scattered haphazardly in the usual prehistoric way and dotted around them are red termite mounds with small sandcastle caps in the local termite style.

The fluffy clouds above catch a lot of this redness and the occasional distant volcanic growths - once stirred up long ago by restless tectonic plates, with their peaks sliced off - are red too.

The first flowers to show in this spring of world prize-winning amazement are the Sturt Desert Pea, which is always the first off the starting line in these parts if the weather is hot enough, a sort of vine which spreads out at great length with a delicate black bloom standing in its deep red heart like a small orchid. There are already patches of them everywhere – they seem to grow before your very eyes – romping tides of blood, announcing the great glories of this coming season, before dying again.

All across the Bush others wait. The shrubs, plants and trees are all green. We've got every shade of green here. Wherever you look you will see something that's about to happen. Something is about to turn. Something else is waiting for the first reviving kiss of rain.

Your first clue as to what is about to take place comes with rows of light blue shoots standing against the green. The very earth is like a maze with shoots readying to spring forth. Oh yes, something is about to take place all right; something really spectacular is about to burst forth. They call it Spring.

A shaft of sun breaks through the wandering clouds and highlights a yellow flower alone in the green bush. You look some more and see some more. The very yellowness of the flowers blaze furiously and they all begin lighting up as if for a wedding. Yellow is such a soft sweet colour, telling us stories of happy endings and marriages which will last no matter what. We put yellow ribbons around the old oak tree to welcome loved ones back from wars. We also think of that old mystic William Blake who saw the world in a grain of sand and heaven in a wild flower.

You shut your eyes and start seeing hundreds, if not thousands, of yellow buttercup heavens. Get ready for the wedding of the year.

***

We drop below the Tropic of Capricorn, still speeding down the coastal highway, and find the verges are covered with romping carpets of white everlastings which are maybe three or four feet deep and go on for miles. The road becomes a huge and brilliant pathway to heaven and we are finding other colours in the white everlastings. This is a pink starflower, my flower book tells me, and that's a golden kangaroo paw.

A row of watching acacia trees are in yellow bloom with some of their yellow blossoms already falling. Their flowers seem to dance in different ways depending on the winds. One minute it's a slow breathy samba, all heaving bosoms and beckoning hips but, when the winds pick up, they're off on a wild, punk dance, every limb jerking and branches thrown around epileptically, shooting out tiny storms of yellow blossom which are gathering in yellow circles around their roots.

Next there's a big bang of blue in the Bush; not just any blue either but the biggest, bangiest blue you have ever clapped eyes on, running a huge carpet of blue away from the road and into the trees. These are scented blue orchids and you must be very careful indeed if you want to take a closer look at them since they seem to be guarded by extremely nasty flies who will attack you, even getting right up your nose and into your ears. These are our flowers they are saying. Geroff.

Liz has been gunning the accelerator a bit because we want to get to Geraldton before dark. These roads are no fun to drive on after dark particularly with those road trains still storming up and down them, even at night, daring anyone to get in their way. But now, in the setting sun, something extraordinary happens in this extraordinary land and again we can't quite believe it.

We have been travelling through hundreds of miles of Bush, relieved only by the wild flowers, but with a lot of the trees charred and dying after being hit by yet more Bush fires. Now, without any warning, the very ground erupts with new and fresh growth with bigger trees, bigger wild flowers and whole fields of yellow oil-seed rape, all telling the same story of a plentiful supply of water hereabouts. The wild flowers themselves have become tremendous, getting twice as big with eye-bursting blues and purples and indigo, displaying themselves proudly on the verges in the dying light. Even the road itself seems to change, getting all twisty, reminding us of the roads in the fragrant mountains of North Wales.

***

After Geraldton we moved inland to Mullewa, a tiny town which nearly became rich in the Gold Rush until many hopeful early prospectors discovered there was no gold there. The town only discovered a decent water supply back in 1950 and now earns a living of sorts as the start of the West Coast wildflower trail.

We are up early, along with the flies, to take one of their dedicated wildflower trails and it again proves quite breathtaking following a woodland path and seeing millions – and I do mean millions – of pink, white and gold pompoms or everlastings all standing to attention with their faces turned upwards at the rising sun. They all stand around so perfectly you would swear they were all put there at simply enormous expense. Aborigines call them ugudungo. Spider orchids are dotted about too, stunning in their elegance and there is something really special – and rare - out these ways called a wreath flower which does look like a funeral wreath except it is a hundred times more beautiful if only because it's real.

I thought of that poetry competition in Spain where the third prize was a silver flower, the second prize a gold flower and the first prize a real flower.

Not quite yet in flower were the pincushion plants, otherwise known as resurrection plants since they will fail in extreme heat or drought like the others and it only needs a small drop of rain to bring them storming back to life.

The resurrection plants. The wreath flower. Mmm. I can't be alone in seeing the clear emblems of Christ mirrored in this wonderful creation of wildflowers which we have surrounded ourselves with in the last few weeks. Neither can I be alone in seeing his stinging crown of thorns and the way his red blood poured down his body to fertilise this red earth.

Oh aye, we're back to red again.

I've always found this concept of the continual death and resurrection of Christ being mirrored in the land very attractive and moving: the way he keeps dying every year to bring forth new life; the way he promotes new growth everywhere with his very blood: the way he will help us live more abundantly if we look at all his wild flowers with eyes that see.

We farewelled him with that terrible crown of thorns but today he is with us, all around us again, with these huge drifts of wild flowers with which he blesses us annually. The one real question is how will we greet him when he does come among us again – as he will if he's not already here. So watch out for him in every sunset and think of him as you look at every wild flower. Prepare yourselves for the return of this wonderful hippy in sandals, my beloved Aussies. He won't be difficult to spot, stepping through a sunlit woodland like this perhaps with a smile on his lips even though he will know he will certainly be roughed up far worse than when he was last with us.

You'll know him when you see him for sure. He will look every inch the Son of Man and will certainly be wearing a crown of wild flowers.

26: Benedictines should tackle the problem of Aboriginal Alcoholism

It is a bright dawn in a monastery garden and I am sitting here with a hangover so thick you could carve slices off it.

I came here to look at the state of my soul and here I am wondering if I'm going to be sick over their flowers. This is my first real hangover for more than two years and I just can't believe I've got into this mess. It's those monks I blame: they should be leading by example, not offering free drinks when you're not looking.

We are in the Benedictine Mission of New Norcia, a jumble of church and monastic houses which forms its own village and community in the gentle hills of Western Australia just above Perth. It was founded 150 years ago and was a rare example, in Australian history, of whites and Aborigines coming together to build the place. The Aborigines received homes, education and health care for their work.

Now two flocks of white parakeets are flying overhead and, in the awful amplification of my hangover, they sound like fifty or so bagpipes warming up - and I hate bagpipes. Huge road trains roar through this village like an almost continual procession of armies heading for war. From somewhere in the monastery come several runs of bells sounding to my hungover ears like the clanging chimes of doom, as Bono once had it.

Yup, I'm going to be sick over those flowers all right.

You can stay here in the monastery guesthouse remarkably cheaply for which they also throw in three meals a day. Men and women do however have to share the shower room, where one of the male guests once bumped into a half-dressed nun, and there is a notice on the door begging for it to be kept closed to keep out goannas, those giant lizards that like to perch on your head. Allegedly…

The food is remarkably vile by any standards and, although I didn't know it when I sat down, they also throw in free wine which wasn't bad and perhaps detracts from the food. I have been nursing my sobriety for a long time now but I must admit I fell, and fell like a stone, when a German space worker sat next to me and filled up my glass which, without thinking, I drank.

We recovering alcoholics all know how one drink's enough, two is too many and three is not nearly enough. And when I lifted up the glass I broke several other rules of sobriety as laid down by Alcoholics Anonymous, namely: Don't pick up the first drink and you won't get drunk, stay sober a day at a time and always avoid drinking situations.

Aided and abetted by the German and others around the table we duly drank the second bottle. Then the German went off and found another bottle in the monastic kitchen and I was pretty soon all over the place and we were all telling daft stories, especially one woman who loved talking about football and another extremely funny woman who suffered from Tourette's when she was stressed and was once in charge of security, complete with a peaked hat, in a diamond mine. "Oh they got away with a few now and then but we watched them like hawks."

We had our own bedroom in the guesthouse but I told Liz I'd stay in the rig in the monastery garden – there had been a few issues between us lately about snoring – and once I'd got in there I found one of her bottles of red which she thought she had hidden – and glugged the lot. There was another one too hidden away in the bathroom too, which I found, and I'm not sure if I drank that but I probably did.

Now I've got this total disgust with myself: hands shaking like a pair of demented butterflies and about to have lunch with the Prior and an interview with him afterwards, all arranged early yesterday just after we'd arrived and I was still stone cold sober. What could I ask him in this mess? How could I write a shorthand note of our encounter? I can't even understand my shorthand when I'm steady.

***

Lunchtime duly comes and it is conducted in silence while one of the monks in a pulpit gives a reading from the book of Benedict about what makes a good monk. I notice all the monks have a half bottle of wine each to accompany their lunch and the organist manages to down three full glasses of a red, which would have got me rocking and rolling all over again, had I tried to keep up with him. Which I didn't.

All the monks finish their wine and, when we join the Prior afterwards in his parlour, the first thing he does is offer us a port. What exactly is going on in this place? Our interview starts and, to make matters worse, the Prior has such a soft voice I barely catch a word he says. I start by apologising for the state I'm in and tell him I've lost a few years sobriety in his cloisters and ask were all Benedictine monasteries like this?

"Oh sure," he beams. "They're always at it in Germany where, after the first course, they come up with whole barrels of beer and cider. But we mustn't get drunk or we might even be asked to leave. What you should have done was top up your wine with the same amount of water. You'd have been all right then. And what is more you seem to be blaming us for your state."

I'm well off my game and ask him rather feebly how the monastery is getting on. "Well we're struggling to get the right type of people and could do with at least 25 more monks. We've even had to stop making our own wine due to difficulties with increased salinity of the local water. But we get by and are concentrating more on hospitality."

"You famously set up this place in partnership with the Aborigines all that time ago. What happened to them? I don't see any black faces anywhere."

"Oh, they just drifted away. There was no falling out. They just went missing and I'm not sure where they are."

***

After leaving New Norcia we continued to the campsite of Perth Vineyards where I have been hatching a proposal to the Benedictine community which may well not be much of a proposal but I'm going to make it anyway.

I think few understand what's happening to the Aborigines because of the grog but, having been on the road in Australia with my reporter's eyes, I am in a position to report the news is bad. There's a lot of trouble brewing in the Northern Territories in particular with fights everywhere and the hellish story, which I told earlier in this book, of the fifty or so young Aborigines – the children of drunken and abusive parents – who had hung themselves.

Aborigines fight in the cemeteries of Broome, openly break the windows of shops and smash caravan windscreens. Many appear to have tried to help them but their approach is piecemeal and I don't think they understand what an appalling, controlling disease this alcoholism is.

Apart from the grog the Aussies have also unleashed an appalling wave of violence on the Aborigines through their worthless, violence-loving television and news services. People who have always lived in communities, with a strong culture and strict rules, hundreds of miles from anywhere and who have always fed themselves by hunting and fishing, can now go home and sit in front of televisions which not only teaches them the foulest language but also tells them – on an almost hourly basis - of drive-bys in Los Angeles, serial killers in Belfast and race riots in Alabama.

If they have Rupert Murdoch's Foxtel television service they are soaked in this evil so how would you expect these simple, poorly educated people to behave with their minds hourly packed with such imagery all further complicated by the grog? It's some small wonder many of them are alive at all, given the nature of their teachers and what they are allowed to drink. When you look at the drunken Aborigines of Broome, fighting one another and encouraging their children to join in, it all makes sense. They are behaving in the manner of what they are seeing every night on their television screens and they have lost control of themselves because of their addiction to the grog.

Yet how simply wonderful it would be for us all if New Norcia could reinvent itself and honour its roots by turning itself into a

Centre for Aboriginal Alcoholism to sell their new students the message that all grog will ever do for them is slowly kill them. Clear teaching on what happens when violence is continually poured onto their hearths would also be a big help.

By attracting leading figures and specialists to their new centre – a kind of holy Betty Ford Clinic – they could easily put this problem on the national and even world agenda. The only way to cure this illness is to get those who are suffering to understand what exactly it is. We also need to know who is profiting from making these gentle, vulnerable people so ill.

The country or world wouldn't be able to ignore the problem – as they seem to now – if the Benedictines, with all their undoubted prayerful power, pitched into the argument and set up a beacon of curative light in a dying poisoned world. People still listen to what Benedictines have to say; they still have our respect although, of course, they too might have to give up the grog themselves, which might be easier said than done by the look of a few of them.

27: Papa is a Rolling Stone

After eight months of seamless sunshine, stretched right across a blue sky every morning, it came as a bit of a shock after leaving Perth to see a cloud. You had to check your eyes were working properly but there it was, lying there like some shapeless, semi-black sun worshipper and, what is worse, another started lying next to it, even blacker than the first.

It got chilly, then we got rain and that was even weirder with these great lusty showers pouring down on everything: over the gum trees and the sheep out in the rich green fields, over the roads and the wild flowers surging up on the verges, on the mighty road trains and the passing cars where the rain kept getting trapped in their speeding wheels like angry, tangled ghosts.

You sense everyone out there is now making plans to travel north in these times of cold and rain. Most of the grey nomads are either in Broome or Darwin or diving into some remote part of the Bush and setting up camp - often to the annoyance of the Aborigines - and staying put there for months on end. This is a source of great irritation to many other nomads as well as the Aborigines. It seems small groups of Grey Nomads go into the Bush together and take over an idyllic spot next to a river or something equally idyllic and stay put, blocking everyone else out.

Every few weeks one will go to the nearest town to get water and provisions and then return to the same spot to share with others until they need something else. Thus they manage to park in ways that make it impossible for any outsider to join them. It's a shame really that they have to eat or they would never go anywhere. But there are always exceptions to every rule, particularly with the Grey Nomads who are all rather exceptional anyway.

I first spotted Michael Blake driving his rackety bus on to a dusty site in Western Australia with his huge savage-looking dog sitting on the passenger seat, watching events closely. Michael had a thick tangle of black hair, which had never seen the working edge of a comb, a grease-stained cap and the alert air of a Bushie who had to keep an eye on everything around him lest some beastie might strike out and take a big bite out of him. He had been on the road since 1988, he said. His bus was his only home and he wasn't like the other so-called nomads who immediately ran home to their big houses as soon as they developed a sniffle.

He had been married to an Irish woman and had two children both now in their thirties, he explained. They all regarded him as an unreconstructed rolling stone but they somehow or other managed to send him a birthday card every two years or so. He hadn't heard from his wife, though, since they parted decades ago. She's Irish, he nodded, as though that somehow explained everything you might ever want to know about his failed marriage.

Their life together had gone reasonably well until the day she announced she wanted to go and live on the roads of New Zealand. That did it for him. He always thought New Zealand roads were rubbish, particularly compared to the wonderful Aussie highways and, to make her proposal far worse, he had never met a Kiwi he liked. He was an out and out Australian, proud to be part of Team Australia - as the then Prime Minister Tony Abbott had been calling it. The other problem with New Zealand was that it was full of Poms (an interesting name which, I have just learned, derives from Prisoner of her Majesty which was tattooed on the arms of British convicts when they were dumped on these shores back in the 1880s.)

I had already heard of Michael from another traveller who had spotted him in a remote part of the Bush making one hell of a racket since he had set up his music speakers outside his bus and was scaring the hell out of the local snakes. He had some Italian opera on at full blast and was conducting it with both arms under the stars for the enjoyment of his sole companion, the dog. The watching travellers didn't stop apparently because they thought Michael was a little terrifying, which he sure is.

Oh, I've always got music and words going wherever I am, he said. He had always been a bit of a techno geek and he really did like being on his own. The only time he and his dog came to campsites was to charge up his batteries and download films off BitTorrent.

This downloading stuff off BitTorrent was news to me. Even as a proud owner of a laptop and dongle I don't know the difference between downloading a film and a poke in the eye - and I suspect it's illegal anyway - but Michael explained that all you need is a steady supply of electricity. A film can take ages to download but, if you are ever moved on, you can always pick up the download later where you left off. He also downloads audio books from somewhere and, despite his apparent loneliness, manages to fill his hours with images and words from elsewhere all the long day through. So maybe he's not lonely at all.

(I have since learned that more than half of Australians now, somehow or other, manage to download their films illegally and pay nothing for them.)

"But my heart really is only in Australia; it's the only country I ever want to live in. I've had some of my most wonderful moments in the gold fields. I can fix almost anything on my bus but, if ever I need an actual spare part, which is real money, I'll go off and pan for gold for as long as it takes. The other place I always enjoy is the Kimberley waterfalls."

Michael wasn't very lovable, I thought, and neither was his nutty, insecure dog who always looked pretty desperate to bite someone and was, it just so happens, part Doberman, the favoured dog of the Nazi concentration camps. "No one would get out alive if they tried to pinch his cushion on the bus and certainly not if they tried pinching one of his bones," Michael said.

But I liked him well enough while being very careful not to go anywhere near the dog's bones or his pillow. Michael was a one-off, I decided, a supreme soloist and rolling stone, comfortable in his own skin and opinions. A true star of the Bush.

28: Revelations of Thunder in an Ordinary World

We next came to rest in the Blue House, a wonderful B&B with six bedrooms on the prow of a hill where parrots fight cockatoos in the garden and I swear I saw a tiny finch with a blue head run up a tree trunk backwards.

Come the dusk and a dozen or so kangaroos with their joeys wander out to graze on the lawns after a long day snoozing in the nearby woodland. They are such lovely things these roos with their fat long tails trailing behind them. I love the way they often sit upright looking around them with their little hands resting on their fat bellies.

Roos are easily spooked though and, if you go too near them, they simply bounce away at speed – boing, boing, boing – and if you are ever wondering why there are so many kangaroos in Australia it's because they can bounce over any fences that you put in front of them with one big boooooooiiiinnnng, their joeys following closely behind.

I don't think I have ever come across a garden so beautiful and interesting as the one Mike and Sue Pickup have put together in their Blue House.

We are in the small town of Nannup in the south west corner of Australia, a straggle of shops, bars and town hall dotted around a main road which looks as though it could be a part-time film set - which indeed it has been. No big city postures here. Everything you look at enshrines all the perfection of the ordinary. This is the archetypal small town, where if you find yourself forgetting what you're doing, someone else will know, rather like our own small town of Bala in North Wales which we are beginning to miss quite badly.

Plan A was to stay in the Blue House for two days which turned into ten. Who could fail to be beguiled by this town? There are trees everywhere, a few churches and right at the end of the main road sits a long-dead steam locomotive clearly destined to stay parked there right up until the end of time.

Our welcome was warm and immediate and we were taken to a pizza place in the main street on our first night where we were put so close to the band I managed to have a long chat with the singer – when he wasn't actually singing - almost right through his set. The band played a lot of lovely golden oldies like Pink Floyd's Comfortably Numb and James Taylor's Fire and Rain and I again began thinking how remarkably old-fashioned most Australians were, certainly in their musical tastes.

The last concert I saw on the road out here kicked off with Buddy Holly's Peggy Sue which is almost as old as me. The endless ads on television are clearly aimed at the older generation and seem to be overtaken by insurance ads promising to pay you a goodly sum for illnesses or sudden death. Who's worried about dying? Well the Australians are for sure.

They were having a film festival here in Nannup when we were around and I went to see a few of the offerings in the town hall. They were pretty dire, rather like most modern films, ridiculous fantasies for the most part flooding the world with perversion and violence. Along with television news - which travels the world at the slightest sniff of violence – both industries are now attacking the world and everyone in it with a simply terrifying hatred.

But, as I have already noted, I see something Biblical in this: we are living in end times and the film and television industries have become the very motors of the monsoons of black rain sweeping the world. These industries drive God mad and I certainly don't want to be anywhere near Hollywood - or any other place where they make films - when he does decide he's had enough and is going to do something about it.

The grave sin of the film industry and indeed television news is that there is no reality in their offerings. When art loosens its grip on the ordinary and particular it becomes worthless. A moment of reality is a moment of truth and, where there is truth, so too there is God.

But the interesting feature for me in the Nannup film festival was that almost no one turned up for their free offerings. People here weren't interested in what the film world had to say. They just wanted to stay at home and enjoy life, and this was a useful insight for me. Real people in a real world have no interest in fantasies of eroticism and violence. They see no value in it and indeed a lot of harm but, as in so many other countries in the world, such people have no voice.

Meet Councillor Murray Cook from nearby Bunbury who showed that his grasp of the ordinary is so keen I wanted to seek him out and hug him. They are putting a municipal dump site in the centre of Bunbury which, for those who don't know, is somewhere where you can dump your toxic fecal matter from your van into a separate drain, usually on a caravan site, straight into the sewers. Mr Murray told the local newspaper he is proud – yes, proud – of this new dump site of theirs. "Bunbury is not on the map and this will do it. It just doesn't matter what it is."

***

After the rain came heavy storms which erupted over Nannup furiously. First the lightning: not tiny forks but huge blamming stammerings of the stuff which lit up every nook and cranny of the surrounding countryside - even the big, brown eyes of the kangaroos who were all looking out from their woodland shelters. That thunder was like no other thunder; loud cracks and rumbles which kept rolling on and on over the heavens like some endless amplified game of skittles.

I have written before of how we can think of God as using the language of monsoons and hurricanes to talk to us and here he is talking to us again in Nannup, clearing up all darkness with the furious insights of his lightning. He sees and understands everything this God of ours and what irks him the most is that those who are responsible for all these storms of black rain always present themselves to us as our allies and friends.

But let there be no misunderstanding on this issue. In its rejection of everything ordinary and real our violence and perversion-loving media has become the world's new tyranny, taking us straight to hell and all of it rotten to the core.

29: A Trojan Horse Tramples Over Our Lives

Squally showers rained down on us as we moved to Esperance, a town known as the Entry to the Goldfields. The place is overwhelmingly charming with great beaches and strange monuments although you would need to be a trained mountain climber to get up and down the cliffs on many of the beaches. One monument, a mad replica of Stonehenge, seemed to be made out of grey plastic and looked like something stolen off the set of Spinal Tap.

My Grey Nomads have disappeared totally - they always appear to be better at avoiding bad weather than us and will probably all be basking in warm sunshine on a beach somewhere where you don't need oxygen cylinders to climb up off it. I met two of them a few weeks ago and they told me they were so slow getting away from the freezing, wet south this year they ended up with flu. They were not about to make that mistake again.

On our third night here we caught the tail end of a tornado in the rig with winds bouncing us around on our beds as if on trampolines and the rain absolutely banging down on the roof. The electricity on the site failed too.

That was all bad enough but a bird living in a tree overhanging us was busy bugling its tiny brains out all night long. He never paused for a single breath or thought, just kept whistling the same barmy phrases again and again with such triumphant verve you would swear he had just won a war single-handedly or that Angelina Jolie had just left Brad and agreed to marry him.

So I got up in the foulest mood only to discover that Liz was in much the same state since a bunch of viruses had attacked our laptop and kept bringing up advertisements for the programs she needed to delete before she could get going. Her every attempt at deletion just made things worse and there was a lot of sighing and un-Liz-like bad language.

We'd been attacked like this a few years ago when a notice came up on our screen telling us that the West Yorkshire Police had closed our computer down because they had found porn on it. The only way to get our computer to work again was with a payment of £100. But we had never downloaded any porn, unlike the majority of people it seems. My son Steffan once worked in a large repair shop where they fixed faulty computers and he said most of the computers they worked on had some kind of porn hidden away on them. The workforce there took it in turns to read it.

We got a techie back home in Bala to sort this West Yorkshire "police" threat out but it was all such a humiliating exercise because the hackers clearly knew so much and we so little. They'd sent in a Trojan Horse, he explained, and it had remained inside the computer for maybe six months before becoming active and playing havoc with our lives. It was all just a con.

I recently learned of another malicious Android app which offered pornography and secretly took pictures of those viewing it with the phone's front facing camera. Then the app made a demand of £330. This method of extortion was yet another example of the most recent malware.

Now I can't function without a computer.

***

When I first became a writer some thirty years ago with my first travel book, Merlyn the Magician and the Pacific Coast Highway – a celebration of bicycling in different capital cities of the world - the work was first scribbled in pencil or any Biro that hadn't run out, on anything from a notebook to the backs of bus tickets. I would come back from bicycling in foreign cities with bags full of stuff. Then I needed to have every typewritten page perfect – if there was a correction or a spelling mistake I would type it all over again. But not any more.

I will still quarry for original work with a pencil and notebook – but now it all gets shovelled into a computer where it is largely corrected onscreen and, with a press of a button, it whizzes off into outer space somewhere and often ends up on a disc on which all corrections can be briskly and painlessly made. I think, but I'm not sure.

I didn't take to the computer immediately. Back in the 1980s Liz bought me an Amstrad and left it on my desk. If truth be told I was scared stiff of it and didn't touch it for a year or so. But then I began a new novel on the Amstrad and, even after accidentally deleting a lot of stuff with the careless press of the wrong button, I can't ever see myself returning to the bad old days of scraps of paper and bus tickets. I don't think there is any loss of quality on a computer either: rubbish in and rubbish out seems to be a perfect and self-evident truth.

***

But today I can't put in rubbish – or get it out – even if I wanted to because a hacker has jammed it solid with threats and demands for money so Liz has gone off to the local computer shop here in Esperance where they have cleaned up the viruses, installed a firewall and promised we will have no more trouble like this. It all cost A$400, which is quite tasty, but, at the very least, the repair has made us both happy again – even with that damned bird still bugling away about how happy he is at the prospect of living with Angelina.

30: The Cost of that Bastard Gold

A red sun is rising on a clear blue sky still holding on to a crescent moon, outlining the severe black geometry of the pithead, more than 100 years old, but today silent, still and dead. A huge open mine is sitting directly next to us but this dead one in front of me is the Sons of Gwalia gold mine in Leonora, founded by two Welsh businessmen and once the fourth biggest in Australia and run, as a young man, by Herbert Hoover who went on to become President of the United States of America.

All around us is a rugged flat countryside whose features are being slowly revealed by the swelling morning light. There is a scattered collection of cacti and long abandoned cars, a group of old corrugated cottages and battered shops, all of which have recently been oldavated into antique slums while other parts of the landscape are dotted with big and small mine workings where desperate men came with their dreams of digging yellow fortunes straight out of the ground with just a shovel. Hoover, who had a way with words, described this land as being of red dust, black flies and white heat.

Some of the early prospectors, if they were lucky, could pick up gold nuggets straight off the ground which could make them a million pounds a week. There's still plenty of it left - though not actually lying on the ground - and today fossickers can still make a lot in their holidays. Wishsticks, the locals call them.

More noises are coming from the working mine next door and there is a hooter telling of the end of a shift. But I am interested in the men now trudging up the hill towards me, all dressed in their normal working clothes and carrying snap tins, billy cans and helmets. Many have beards, not because beards are seen as smart or sexy but because water is always short around here, particularly hot water and some men need an awful lot of it to shave.

Yet for miners they are remarkably smartly dressed. Agnes Devlin said that her "Grandma an' Papa used to take in washing and ironing. A lot of the men looked to have their good shirts and things washed and ironed for work."

Many of the workers have just come from the old corrugated houses at the bottom of the hill. These houses have the traditional ill-fitting windows and tamped down earth for floors. The walls are of hessian, and looking very rough nowadays, and the garden fences are made of old bedsteads and other scrap.

"People in the cottages used kerosene fridges when they first came out here, but before that they had coolers and hurricane lamps and kerosene lights," said Bob Crofts.

They've also restored the prison. "Gwalia was a bit like a Wild West frontier town. If you were trying to maintain law 'n' order you had to be physically prepared to back up what you said," Constable Bob Primrose recalled.

"I am from the Darlot people, Kaora language group," said Joan Tucker. "In the 1950s and 60s, my father, Jim Brennan, worked here for the Sons of Gwalia. He had been a Rat in Tobruk and learned to speak Italian as a prisoner of war in Italy. I went to Gwalia school where I most enjoyed inter-school sports, especially with the Mount Margaret Mission kids."

Yet more men are joining the early shift – Italians mostly who have always formed the bulk of the workforce. Unlike the Italians of popular myth these men are quiet and thoughtful since they are about to start a shift down this incredibly dangerous mine.

The list of deaths in this mine makes grim reading. One man was suffocated after being buried in eight tons of sand. Danny Tait died of a heart attack and another committed suicide with the help of a stick of gelignite. Another had his every artery cut after being sucked into a machine. The price of gold, they always said. Oh yes, the price of that bastard gold.

The horses were treated better than the men: they had two stable hands looking after them, keeping the stables free of cockroaches and mice. Those horses were well fed and taken up regularly for fresh air and exercise. "They had millions of cockroaches down there which would make whole walls move. Most of the roaches were white because all the colouring had gone out of them through lack of sunlight and the horses used to eat them," said Tom Straw, a former Gwalia miner.

The miners themselves fought off all diseases by drinking plenty of beer, champagne and the local grog in the local sly grog shops. Drink was their answer to all ailments. When in doubt get legless.

The men moved into a cage which dropped them 2,500 feet, soon out with their drams and horses and busy at the face, filling up a dram an hour which was washed and processed in the mine buildings above where, under watchful eyes, they extracted the gold.

My men are all ghosts of course, sounds without echoes: small sad arias from a long lost season in hell. But they are still here. You can still sit here and hear them again; you really can reach out

185

and touch them. A local wishstick proudly showed me buckshot he had dug up with which they used to shoot rabbits for food.

These ghosts should be seen as authentic Australian heroes, stars of the goldfield who, like my ancestral miners in Wales, first dug out a big part of their country's considerable wealth. Yes, they all paid heavily for their work, many with their lives.

31: Our New Tyranny is Pushing Us Into War

I have always been fascinated by the lives of underground miners, perhaps because I come from a coal mining family myself. My grandfather died as a young man in a pit explosion in Ynysybwl mine in the valleys of South Wales and my father also worked briefly down the same hole before becoming a bricklayer in the steelworks in Cardiff. Safer, he said, and he lasted well beyond eighty. I went to live with the striking miners of the Rhondda for two years in 1983/4 as they fought to keep their pit open and where I set my most successful novel, Black Sunlight.

Now having just finished touring the goldfields of Australia I can see all too clearly how they have all fallen into the same social problems. In both countries we can see the same high street dereliction: the same closed and boarded up shops: the same ubiquitous charity shops everywhere (I bought ten washed and beautifully ironed handkerchiefs in a charity shop in Norseman for a dollar) and the same empty pubs often run by embittered landlords who just want to sell them off and retire to somewhere near the sea where they can live out their remaining days fishing while their wives sat in their cars making sandwiches for lunch.

But the buildings most difficult for me to look at in both countries are the empty churches and chapels, the pews empty and pulpits sold for firewood. The shells just sit there in sad clouds of vanquished glory, I always like to think, dreaming empty dreams of another revival.

The main feature of these dispirited streets – for me anyway – are the one-eyed television satellite dishes, everywhere the emblems of a corrupt new tyranny which now rules the world with an iron fist – both here in Australia and in Wales and everywhere else – all turning the clean rain of heaven into a murderous black rain wherever they are operating, pouring out their sulphurous messages of death and destruction both in films and news.

Here in Australia every hearth has become contaminate with this evil. You will also see the influence of our fallen film industry in most modern crimes when you know where to look. Its peculiar and destructive darkness is always in there somewhere.

***

During my years with the South Wales miners I kept a close watch on the visiting television cameras; they turned up whenever there was the slightest hint of trouble and persistently exaggerated it, making Margaret Thatcher more determined than ever to crush the miners. She was also clearly an avid watcher of television news and was always going on about what she had seen on the news the night before as if it were gospel.

But today our bloodthirsty media has considerably raised the stakes since those awful beheadings took place in the Middle East and, tragic and horrible as they were, we have now got into the situation where half of Australia is afraid to go to the shops to buy a loaf of bread for fear of having their heads chopped off.

The Islamic population in the Australian cities is also fearful of being attacked leading to a situation rather like the forty years of bloodshed in Northern Ireland. The media was well behind that ongoing disaster; they always fastened on to small outbreaks of trouble and set fire to them to the extent that few knew who they were fighting or why. And all the trouble was always in the poor, unemployed areas. When it came to sectarian rioting you could always rely on the uneducated, the ignorant and the stupid on all sides to scrum down together. Educated, middle-class areas were free of trouble.

Now the US, Britain and Australia is bombing the Middle East in the hope of destroying the ISIS militants and their ideas, clearly hoping to make them think again before beheading another. As if. As lost causes go this might be the lostest and again the news media is firmly behind all this.

I know how the media works because I once worked for the best of them. I also know how they destroyed the Welsh miners because I was there when it happened. I get it and, when you have finished reading this book, you too I hope will understand how incredibly evil this media is and how it will sooner or later usher us into a new world war unless we somehow find a way to stop it.

✳✳✳

We need to go back to 2013 when two Islamists attacked and tried to behead a soldier, Lee Rigby, in broad daylight in Woolwich, London. When Michael Adebolajo finished his murderous attack, still with blood on his hands, he took a camera phone off a passer-by and explained why he had done it. Onlookers used their own phones to post updates of this horrific scene which lasted 16 minutes and was posted in real time around the world. There were no television cameras present at the incident and Adebolajo just addressed the smart phones of bystanders. What he was doing, in effect, was to stage the world's first electronic press conference at the scene of the crime.

"The only reason we have killed this man is because Muslims are daily being killed by British soldiers," he told a passing Blackberry, his bloodied hands still clutching a meat cleaver. His views were recorded at 2.30 in the afternoon and within minutes were on ITV News. The film-maker had been rushed by taxi to the television company's headquarters 11 miles away.

Another local resident held a cameraphone out of his flat window recording the two men waiting for the police without even attempting to run away. That footage was shown on the net throughout the world within seconds. The BBC and ITV received 800 complaints about their coverage, many distressed by the air time the murderers received to explain their views.

But their views had already flown around the world; this new storm of black rain had swept every country in every land and even the judge at the duo's subsequent trial was moved to announce that Rigby's murder had clearly been got up for the benefit of the media.

***

We now move on to the ISIS media headquarters in the Middle East, always busy posting quite sophisticated footage about jihad on the net which is widely used particularly by SBS television here in Australia and watched – and reported on - by the Press.

But the Woolwich attack had rewritten the script. In terrorist terms it would have been a total success and what they needed now, the terrorists will have concluded, was something truly horrible, something which will also sweep the world though a supine media, with a frightening ferocity.

Simple really. We'll dress someone up in a Satanic black, call him Jihad John, let him deliver a few words of propaganda and get him to behead a journo or two. That would make everyone sit up. And it did. All over the world and all of it straight out of the gospel according to Michael Adebolajo.

Jihad John's murders also worked like the very greatest terrorist dream and within days political leaders everywhere were denouncing John and co. while planning to rain down bombs on these monsters hiding behind their sand dunes and beginning a war which could last for years and no one could win.

The only feature you need to understand about modern terrorism is that they are always after three things: publicity, publicity and publicity. They are forever dreaming of new ways to garner this publicity and, thanks to a media which always rolls over at the prospect of violence, we can be sure that we have seen nothing yet. What next? Live babies impaled on spikes? We've already seen a young child in Australia holding up the severed head of a man in his hand. Holidaymakers have been slaughtered on a beach in Tunisia. Oh there's another beheading in France and they've left the head on a spike on a gate.

Their latest outrage was a "snuff movie" showing five Muslim men dressed in red jump suits and packed together in a cage which was lowered into a swimming pool with cameras recording their final few minutes as they thrashed around and drowned.

The journalist who commented on this outrage, Jonathan Freedland of the Guardian, neatly illustrated the confusion and hypocrisy of the media when reporting terrorist acts when he wrote: "I rely here on reports (of these drownings). My small stance against the so-called Islamic State's propaganda is to refuse to watch its propaganda."

Well, that's all right then isn't it? He doesn't watch it, in his great and absolutely heroic stand against Islamic propaganda, but finds the space to report in full the details of these drownings to his million odd readers. How can terrorists possibly lose anything when they've got such as Freedland up against them?

The curtain must come down on this evil production which is being staged by the bloodthirsty tyranny of our media and is allowing the mad to take centre stage holding up bloody heads while also giving them a voice, a stage, influence and power. If it's allowed to continue nothing less than the safety and future of the world is at stake and this sacred land of Australia is far too wonderful and important to be left in the hands of such as that scumbag Rupert Murdoch and his thuggish employees.

Murdoch continues to interfere in the political affairs of Australia, the US and the UK with his tweets and it must be said that he has pretty much ruined most of the newspapers he's taken over, including the once-great Sunday Times, now packed with celebrity, sex-obsessed and spiteful garbage with reporters stuck in the newsroom when they were once sent out all over the land to make own their investigations into the issues of the hour.

32: How the Heavens Farted on the Nullarbor

For most of the year the road across the Nullarbor, one of the longest and most dangerous in Australia, which stretches some 2,000 km from West Australia (where we were) to Adelaide (where we wanted to get to), had been hanging over us like a death sentence.

Oh you're going to have to take the Nullarbor, fellow travellers would say. Well good luck. You're going to need it. It goes on for ever, they would go. Get in plenty of stops and sleep a lot. If you come across a kangaroo just run him over. All kinds of trouble follows if you try and swerve out of their way.

But Liz, who honed her rallying skills on the mountains of North Wales, had no fears and was looking forward to it. So we took the road out of Norseman, another somewhat defeated gold mining town, and floored the accelerator daring any kangaroo stupid enough to get in our way.

But oh the road was nose-bleedingly boring; you could see that from the off with very few things to look at unless you happen to like looking at smashed-up bodies of kangaroos which were everywhere. Occasionally you spotted big-eyed emus lurking in the bushes and you slowed right down in case they were in a suicidal mood – which they often were – although it was the huge and beautiful wedge-tailed eagles that you really had to watch out for because they like to feed off carrion and need a lot of wing flaps to gain enough height, particularly to get out of the way of the thundering road trains.

There were dead possums too which at least seemed to die in tidy curled-up balls – and even a few snakes and lizards which hadn't made it to the safety of the opposite verge - but we didn't spot any camels which have lived on these plains for more than a century having been brought in to build the Adelaide railway and other projects and then abandoned out here in the desert. Camels don't need a regular supply of water – for which they were given humps - and will eat anything. I have also learned that camels can't reverse which is why the streets in the towns in Australia are so wide since they needed to be big enough to accommodate a turning camel train.

However not only did we not run over anything we didn't even see anything worth running over. It was a real relief we hadn't managed to flatten a kangaroo so far particularly after one grey nomad had told us how a huge kangaroo came flying through his windscreen, not only managing to stay completely intact but ending up sitting directly between him and his passenger and facing the right way. They both bailed out immediately since kangaroos don't like this happening to them and can get very upset if it does.

Yet the road itself was fine – including a 146 km (90 mile) stretch of completely straight road, the longest straight road in Australia - and we carried on for some 400 km before pulling off at sunset and camping in the Bush which, apart from breezes rustling in gum trees, was as silent as the grave, except for the usual loud argument between us about whose turn it was to make the tea. This argument erupts about four times a day. You'd think two grown-ups would organise something like a rota. But if Liz thinks she is losing the argument she will start going on about how she was certainly well up last month or else, if really desperate, she might even claim that she didn't want any tea after all and she'll just have a glass of squash.

We were on day two down the Nullarbor when the very heavens farted. We had a tyre blow-out and I must say that had I sat down with a map of Australia and a compass I just couldn't have picked a worse place in this whole vast continent – or perhaps even the world – to have a tyre blow-out.

We couldn't get a connection to anyone on the mobile, most crucially to the RAC, because we were too far away from anywhere. And while we may have been carrying a spare tyre I didn't know where it was; and anyway I wouldn't have had a clue how to change it. At first no one was stopping to help and a few even speeded up when they saw us. Then the day smiled on us.

An elderly couple towing a caravan stopped and the man immediately plunged under our rig preparing to get the damaged tyre off. He located our spare and somewhat amazingly said it had air in it but what I shall never forget was the way he was wriggling around on the gravel fixing our tyre, causing cuts on his arms making blood pour down them. His wife stood above him and he did what she told him. We Aussies know all about cars, she explained. We'll get you going.

That truly extraordinary Aussie kindness and helpfulness again. Oh how I have come to love these people.

Oh well, I thought, grovelling with genuine gratitude, we're surely going to get out of this mess now, when a ramshackle bus, with all its wheels pointing in different directions, pulled up and out stepped a really old guy, smiling with a huge set of false teeth which fell down whenever he opened his mouth and laughed. He was accompanied by a rather regal Aborigine and they both came over to help. Now there were a whole row of people under our rig although the Aborigine didn't do or say anything. He had a white towel tied around his head making him look like a pint of Guinness.

There are four back wheels on our rig, one of which was completely stripped of its tread, which they got off. Now the newcomer with the collapsing teeth got the spare in place when somehow – and no one is still quite sure how – he managed to let the neighbouring tyre down and break its valve. So where we once had one dodgy flat tyre we now had two. He did offer to pay for what he'd done but, as no one was sure what he'd done, including him, we refused the offer.

We did somehow manage to get sufficient air into all the tyres to limp into the nearest roadhouse, which revelled in the name of Cocklebiddy, and Liz found a landline to the wonderful RAC who sent out a truck the next morning which towed us the 460k back to Norseman where we were fixed up with two new tyres. I was never so glad to see that RAC truck since we had become pretty convinced we would have to stay in Cocklebiddy eating their terrible, over-priced food until Christmas.

Liz managed all this with her usual calm – she's had plenty of practice in dealing with trouble after fifty years of marriage to me – but I must admit that I had, for the first time, stopped enjoying the journey particularly with the thought that we now had to repeat that 460 km to get back to Cocklebiddy - where we had left off - with a further 1,500 km to go to Adelaide – a total journey of 2,500 km.

***

We did finally manage to clear the Nullarbor five days later with no further incidents and had been deeply fortunate to meet a truly generous couple, Mandy and Malcolm Peace – the M&Ms -

who loaned us their lovely second home on the sea in Port Willunga near Adelaide where I stretched out in a catatonic trance and did nothing on the leather sofa in their living room but stare at the ceiling for two weeks, only moving to go to bed.

I got better on that leather couch and we were ready for whatever came next.

33: A Savage Pilgrimage Beneath a Blood Red Moon

Most long journeys have their ups and downs. There was the disaster on the Nullarbor but, having recovered from that, I am now in a deep dark pit and this journey has become what DH Lawrence once called a savage pilgrimage. I am writing this with my head full of snakes, sitting on a shoreline in Meningie and a big fat pelican is looking at me.

After Willunga we went up into the Adelaide Hills to visit one of my oldest friends, the artist Mary Marston who lives in some splendour in Mount Torrens in a glass-walled house overlooking ten acres of woodland amok with kangaroos and multi-coloured parrots who flutter down through the leaves like falling chunks of rainbows.

Indeed it is the kind of place that one of heaven's gardeners might have come up with after being let out down here on parole for a month.

Trees stand around with hanging branches as if in silent prayer; the lake has become a home for all kinds of birds wanting a drink or a swim and the first light always bejewels the cobwebs thick with dew. Mary enjoys going down to the lake for a bit of a gomp in the middle of the night beneath a sky invariably studded with a glittering wilderness of stars.

We met Mary in Seventies London when I was on the Sunday Times, through her husband, Derek Parkes, who was an old university friend and property developer. When they split up Mary returned to her former home town, Adelaide, where she did some of her own property development, ending up with this fantastic house in the mountains which makes you feel she has found a way of turning the world inside out and laying bare all its secrets. Wherever you sit you seem to be able to see everything there is, even the kangaroos who come out of the distant woodland to eat her flowers, their saucer eyes ablaze with starlight.

A few nights ago a few of us gathered in the garden to watch a rare eclipse of the moon as it passed through the earth's shadow. This blood red moon has become something of a prophecy in its own right; it tells us about the state of the world, many believe, and how we - and everything in it - will soon be changing.

It was so cold I stayed inside the house drinking tea when a film caught my eye on the television listings – Snakes on a Plane. I had never seen it – although I had heard a lot about it – so I turned it on. I see watching all kinds of films as being an important part of my work, even though they often upset me grievously. I would not have understood what had happened in Hungerford, for example, had I not once seen a Rambo film while on holiday in Portugal with my sons trying to avoid the rain and which, for some reason, stayed vividly in my mind.

That's why so many of our so-called experts never know where to look when they are examining events like school shootings in America: they are so clever they have never seen the damned films, many of which started the trouble in the first place.

**

It is extraordinary, I have long thought, how that one key word – romantic – so comprehensively describes the inner workings of our media, particularly our film industry. It is also a word which describes the obsessive search for violence in news gathering; a word which so often aptly describes what's going on in drama while at the same time explaining the media's fevered attachment to perversion and sexual inconstancy.

This word also pretty accurately describes the very heart of Hollywood whose work revels in cruelty, violence and sensationalism of every kind; a place which covers everything from drive-by shootings to school massacres. This word describes the Nietzschean superhero, a man who towers over everyone else and sets out to reshape the world with his own savage criminality. Such superheroes have become the role models of nitwits everywhere who then dress up, find a gun and stage mass shootings in schools and churches. And such massacres are going to become more abundant if only because no one has a single clue what causes them.

Just lately I have learned, as I write this, of a new and grim apotheosis in these shootings on August 15, 2015, when in Maryland, Virginia, a gunman, Vester Flanagan, shot dead a reporter and cameraman on live television. It emerged that Flanagan filmed the attack as it happened which was posted live on the net and immediately went viral. It had all clearly been set up for television and, oh boy, did it work well. He immediately went on the run in his car and, pursued by the police, ended up shooting himself dead.

Thus, another mad moron – in this long and increasingly desperate age of black rain – became world famous with the active help of all his thousands of accomplices in the media with the best technology now available in our 24-hour television news services. Like Isis he knew exactly what to do and how to frighten the world while he was at it. The jihadists know everything about manipulating the media and it hadn't taken Flanagan long to work it out for himself either.

***

Admittedly guided by the learned hand of Mr T S Eliot I had been woken up to this word romantic at an early age in Malaysia and almost throughout my whole life I have seen the extraordinarily accurate way it describes the rings of evil as they encircle and destroy so many in our increasingly beleaguered world. It was but a drizzle when I was young and became a fearsome storm in middle age. Now it is a positive world tsunami, blowing through every corner of our lives, undermining our values, dismissing the claims of reality and telling us, perhaps in not so many words, to re-assert ourselves by leaving our families and children, to glory in the carnal and, when all else fails to achieve our happiness, we might even become super-hero ourselves, resorting to mindless violence, the more mindless and violent the better.

Yes indeed the word romantic does have a pretty wide-ranging role covering a whole host of philosophies and weird stances. Yet it has only ever meant one thing to me which is a translucent fungus growing out of a manuscript with faces and tadpoles of ideas moving around inside it. That is the perverted and poisonous fungus of my own romanticism which I saw in Malaysia. And immediately got rid of.

Indeed there are some who still say that I am a very romantic character who writes romantic books and, if true, I have no defence against that charge although I am now sure that I was a romantic before God had a word with me about it in Malaysia and, in the process, he showed me what he really believed a romantic is – someone basically who is forever in the persistent pursuit of the violent, the perverted, the melancholy and the cruel – a lie which explains fully what drives most of our media and is leading the world into a growing peril and from which there is going to be no escape for any of us.

So when God tossed me out of the barmy fog of romanticism he was giving me my life's calling. When he showed me that vision of black rain he was also showing me a vision of how his world is being derailed and why it is drifting into so much chaos. That black rain is romantic in its source, all of it killing the world through our media rather than nourishing our parched and dying lands with the clean rain of heaven.

God told me all this in one brief, penetrating vision in the Penang sky and now I understand why our cities are becoming the home for so much anarchy and criminality, why terrorism is pulling apart the Middle East and indeed why schoolchildren are being shot in American schools and worshippers in churches.

My visions all add up, they all make perfect sense - to me anyway - although I do admit I have a very long way to go before convincing the rest of the world in what I believe.

**

I am saying all this again because I watched Snakes on a Plane in Mary's place, which is perhaps not the most biting or clever production of Hollywood's. (Nothing like the repellent Alien for example which I once wrote about in the Observer and so upset Ridley Scott he couldn't speak for a day.) But Snakes on a Plane is a good example of a film, I would suggest, which sets out to be comedy but could seriously destabilise a child's mind for a long time and perhaps forever. Almost a year later back home here in Wales all those same snakes are still living in corners of my mind vividly and I really must stop believing that watching such rubbish is part of my job. But how can I otherwise do it?

The story of Snakes on a Plane – insofar as this farrago of nonsense can be said to have a story – involves Samuel L Jackson, an FBI agent, taking a prisoner on a plane when terrorists release hundreds of snakes to cause a diversion in which said prisoner can escape. These snakes bob up from everywhere attacking the passengers and killing them, beginning with a naked couple who are getting down and dirty in the plane's lavatory. For his part Jackson starts zapping the snakes with a stun gun and later a fire extinguisher which really riles the snakes. One comes up the dress of a sleeping woman and goes straight into her eye and kills her. When one of the stewards is attacked he manages to get the snake into a microwave and cooks him. A python attacks the captain in the cockpit and the snake somehow or other finds an open door and flings the poor captain out into deep space. Another passenger throws a small dog at a snake and said dog immediately gets eaten. But the same passenger is punished when an enormous snake decides to eat him. We see this snake engulfing his head with his jaws making it look like a giant condom that's going on the wrong bit. A passenger is drafted in to fly the plane while the captain is still spinning out in space and, of course, this passenger has never flown a plane before but manages to land this one on the tarmac because he's had plenty of practice on his PlayStation.

It is all completely barking and not even funny, as my synopsis might suggest. Jackson throughout brings nothing but the worst of amateur nights to his role and you so wish one of the bigger snakes would have got him at the start of the film and eaten him whole.

Needless to say this trash made a lot of money and the same gang went on to make Snakes on a Train.

**

Later we were all out in Mary's garden looking up at the full eclipse which had made the moon turn red. Even with my mind still disordered with all those snakes I could still appreciate the bold majesty of the moment: a blood sign gazing down on the world, telling them to prepare for momentous happenings. This blood prophecy tells us that the end of the world is coming faster than any of us may have dared believe and, whatever else we may do, we should be ready.

"The sun will turn into darkness and the moon will become as blood," it says in the Book of Joel. "Then the great and terrible day of the Lord will come."

34: Why God Wants the Media to Lay Down its Arms

My savage pilgrimage continued and I still couldn't get rid of all those snakes from my mind and thoughts. My main worry was what effect such a film would have on children who could have seen it easily enough as it was on television at eight o'clock. I even found myself getting quite angry about it all, wondering why they didn't just send tankers full of acid into Australian schools to spray the children while they were out in the playground and be done with it.

But I was also beset by a more general worry about why God allowed all this to go on. He was fast enough dumping all his worries on me about a corrupt media in Malaysia, I would tell myself, as yet another snake slithered down another alleyway of my brain, but why doesn't he address the world directly if he feels that strongly about it? He also could also have surely found someone better qualified to deliver such a message than me. He's got the Pope, he's got the Archbishop of Canterbury and he's even had most of the presidents of the US. They could have just called in the media and told them what was on their minds and expect it all to be published. He might even have got Obama to stop going on about gun control all the time.

He could perhaps have taken some direct action himself by sending a few good hurricanes into Hollywood and erasing the whole area. That would be a good start and it would almost certainly halve the booming murder rate in America.

He might even have blasted al Jazeera television in Doha with a few lightning strikes which would settle down the Middle East no end.

But oh no. Nothing could be less likely. As far as I can see all he's ever done is pick on me leaving me with a headache that's lasted 50 years, except when I've been drunk.

***

But a few days later a new nuisance began running around the Australian news bulletins in the form of Sydney teenager Abdullah Elmir, a teenage white knobhead, who had made a 90-second video – Jihadis are clever and avid video makers - saying that his troops would soon be putting black flags on top of Buckingham Palace and the White House and executing world leaders. He was dressed up like Genghis Khan on a bad hair day clutching an assault rifle and surrounded by a dozen or so other uniformed knobheads all glaring at the camera menacingly and clutching their weapons.

Incredibly this nonsense was featured on the front pages of most newspapers and television news bulletins. Even the then Australian premier, Tony Abbott, seemed to have swallowed it – he was a real gloom merchant who only ever get gloomier - saying it was yet further evidence of the Islamic threat. I can never understand why politicians feel the need to exaggerate the terrorist threat – which they often do – when they've got a media perfectly capable and willing to do that for them.

If this coverage was proof of anything at all, I would say, it told us clearly that our violence-loving media had gone completely potty and had pretty much driven our political leaders potty too.

In fact it is really difficult to tell who is the pottier – the media or the terrorists who constantly lead them around by the nose. This is a marriage straight from hell in which they all satisfy one another's deepest needs and there is no sign at all of a divorce.

But, deep in the Holy Spirit, I am telling you that not only does God want this divorce but that the future of Australia – and even the world - might depend on it. Oh how simply wonderful it would be if Australia could take the lead in all this.

***

Thus I carried on, often feeling as if I were talking to myself, wondering if I had been saddled with this role as a freelance prophet until the end of my days. It was my old pal, the much-missed Canon David Watson who was instrumental in my giving up journalism and devoting my life to books, who always said that I should always try to honour the fire that God had built in me. But David had a huge following and mine is anything but that. I always did the work: it was the following I was missing.

Yet I guess you simply cannot retire from a job like this because you don't feel like doing it any more or you're not happy about the money or extremely doubtful about the career prospects. You just get on with it and keep hoping – praying? – that God will look after you, keep you going somehow and eventually raise up your words as and when and if he finally decides the time is right. When I'm feeling old and beleaguered and when my body does feel it's about to conk out I just have to keep believing he is still there for me – and us - and that he will keep giving me the right words to deal with his enemies.

But, despite my books I've never felt I've got all that far with my message that there are great stirrings in The Kingdom, that the angels are mobilising and that the Man of Lawlessness, a great tide of evil, which I believe to be the modern media, is actually with us and in every home, will soon be exposed and defeated. Then it's The Return.

Yet what I didn't know then was that my floundering career as a freelance prophet was soon going to take a very sharp turn upwards; that I would find – or be given? – a way of making my words something far more than my mere words, all finding an agreeable home in the minds and thoughts of almost a quarter of a million, even perhaps a half a million people depending on the way you count them, giving me a following even bigger than David's.

I simply never knew that at all, and never even suspected it.

35: The Anguished Cries of Drowning Souls

We rested up in the lovely Port Fairy – where they even have their own Port Fairy time which means Whenever – and the kindness of Australians continued to amaze us. The receptionist in the caravan park offered us the loan of her flat for a few weeks because she was going away and we had only known her for fifteen minutes. This spontaneous generosity always touches my pilgrim heart and I can get quite weepy when I hear it.

Then it was the Great Ocean Road and we were driving into one of the wilder paintings of JMW Turner, all boiling mists with foggy red sunsets and the largest waves crashing into – and over – everything. I've always loved huge rolling waves and you can all but hear the conversations between them; arguments about when they are going to knock over the next huge limestone pillar or even bragging about what kind of ships they have taken down over the years. These notions are not entirely fanciful because these same waves tumbled over one of the Twelve Apostles some ten years ago – a great stack of rock, thrusting vertically out of its foaming root - after hundreds of years of determined effort.

And they brought down one of the huge arches of London Bridge on January 15, 1990 on this same shoreline leaving two people stranded on the outer arch. They had to be rescued by helicopter.

And oh those great ships – about 160 of them – all driven by gales and smashed on to rocks on this Southern Ocean shore, with untold numbers of early mariners, immigrants and so many others sinking to their deaths with their drowned bodies rolling around beneath those huge bragging waves. A graveyard for ships they still call this stretch of coast. Records tell of the death by drowning of clippers, windjammers and caravels including a four-masted iron barque which smashed against that red limestone rock there becoming a tourist attraction for six months before breaking up completely.

***

It is said that on quiet summer nights in these splashy coves, when the sky and cliffs are full with a brilliant yellow sunset, you can sit here on the clifftop and listen to the last sounds of those dying souls, all of them rolling around and around with the waves as their cries for mercy were drowned and they reached out for the rescuing arms of their mothers.

At the Twelve Apostles that are left - yet more explosive pillars of ragged beauty - the waves storm against their roots, determined to bring down another pillar. Shearwaters are flying around them ceaselessly, crying out with sheer happiness having just returned from their breeding grounds in the Arctic where they go each year to feed on vast clumps of mosquito larvae.

There are lots of foreign visitors around here today – possibly Jehovah's Witnesses after one of their big conventions in Melbourne last weekend – and everywhere gulls are screaming at them for food. There's no fire danger today, says a sign. Well that's all right then.

We made just about every stop on the Great Ocean Road and every foaming cove filled our eyes with wonder and delight. No matter how hard you looked you just couldn't seem to take it all in although little prepared us for the one final great surprise just before getting into Apollo Bay where we were due to spend the night.

We were looking for Cape Otway Light Station at the end of the road, the oldest surviving lighthouse in Australia, and driving down an endless twisting lane through a forest to get to it when we pulled up in front of a group of Chinese who were all gesticulating excitedly upwards. And there it was. Our year-long search was over. A koala, fat with eucalypt, stretched out on an overhanging branch, fast asleep. Just on the other side of the lane was a baby koala also spark out.

Our joy was unconfined. We had been searching the Bush for these goofballs ever since we had begun this trip and here they were at last. I had long dreamed of holding a koala but, disappointingly, not only were these two fast asleep but they showed no sign of waking up, not even for a good cuddle from me. It was just as well, I was to learn, because they have very sharp teeth and claws which they are not averse to using particularly after being woken up in a bad mood by a wandering pair of Welsh gypsies.

We carried on to see six further koalas, who weren't all fast asleep, but seemed determined not to come near us, still less to climb into our arms. One just sat there grumpily chewing on a few leaves and staring at us without any expression in his brown pebble eyes.

The winding stairs up to the top of the lighthouse were steep and high and once up on the iron walkway, which circled the top of it, the wind kept ripping the very breath out of our mouths. But we hung on to the rail tightly as we walked around, mesmerised by the vast and turbulent views beneath our feet, with the rolling sunlight ever changing all the way to the outlying hills and forests. Within this tumbling light you could see again those first immigrants struggling ashore on the beach with even non-believers calling on God for safe delivery from all this. All this!

I will always remember those transcendent hours of beauty that day atop those sea-stormed coves. I will always be able to walk over them again, in my mind, with my beloved wife in one hand and a tame toothless koala in the other, my very being feeding on those great sea breezes. Even in my darkest hours the memory of this day will transform and sustain us both in our love of this great country which we will both fight for - and defend, and miss - until our own final hours.

36: Wanna be a Famous Superhero and get your face on the telly?

We are currently recruiting for a new terror group based in Sydney and interviews will be taking place over the next few weeks.

This group, whose aims are not yet formulated - except for creating the maximum trouble and fear everywhere - is seeking young men and women who genuinely enjoy manufacturing strife and manipulating the media. This work, we have learned from some of our Middle East members, is extremely easy since all arms of the Australian media are run by people who will do anything you want providing you offer them some form of violence. They will also publish almost anything you bung them as long as there is a bomb – or the promise of a bomb – in it.

The right applicants will be trained in media skills and you will be taught what to say to the media, how to say it and when. For explosions, for example, you will need to ring them just in time for their news deadlines. Journalists have no ability to plan for the future so what you say will always have to come from the Now. There must always be an element of violence in anything you are saying to them, whether this violence is real or imagined or even threatened. The bigger and more lurid the violence the better. This line of work is nothing if not endlessly creative.

Single severed heads are now considered boring and rather predictable in our business, for example, so any applicant who turns up for interview with a sack of freshly severed heads would win immediate favour. This will delight the interviewing panel with your initiative and real seriousness of purpose.

We would also be impressed by any candidate who explained to us how he or she might kidnap a politician, kill him, cook him and then stage a press conference in which, say, five members of our group would actually eat him from head to toe. Oh the hacks would scream and shout a little in their pointless editorials but they wouldn't stop taking their pictures and writing up their news reports. They expect us to be as objectionable as possible. We can always do disgusting at the drop of a hat which is why, deep down, the media really loves us and rewards our skills with such global publicity.

But if the truth be known they don't really care what you do as long as it is newsworthy and has the ability to spread fear in the community. In an ideal world this fear will pit one section of the community against the other – always for reasons few ever understand. We terrorists are the new prophets of racial and religious division and the media has always been – and always will be – our mouthpiece. Without them we would be nothing but they will always be there for us simply because we always give them what they really live for.

The pay for this important new opening in our expanding Sydney office, including the super, will be very good - even if we freely admit you are not expected to last that long, particularly if you are co-opted on to the suicide corps. But you will get your own office, where you can perhaps entertain your media contacts, and there will be many other perks including the use of the office tank for your holidays.

You will be asked to put the office tank to good use if you do take it, with any kids you might have, on your holidays. It is a fully equipped Sherman with its own shells and, while it might get the Army too interested if you started blowing up buildings with it, you could probably do well just by taking it on to the beach in the popular Byron Bay, say, and running over a lot of sunbathers. Now that would be a story which would run everywhere in the world.

You should also know that we also have a spare tank which we keep in a secret base near Darwin serving the Northern Territories which will also be made available for holidays to whoever we hire up there. This is also a Sherman which was stolen and transported home by one of our number in a recent skirmish in Syria.

Indeed the pair of you could even join forces on a sort of terror holiday stunt by coming down to Byron Beach at the same time in the holiday season, coming from each end of the sand in your tanks with black flags fluttering on them. You could then herd the holidaymakers into one big group and proceed to run them over. Many will doubtless try to escape by diving into the sea but we have a tank full of sharks nearby who will not have been fed for a month and will be released just off Byron Bay at the same time as we attack with the tanks. Thus those we do not get run over on the sand will be eaten in the sea.

This stunt would undoubtedly give the survivors a holiday they would never forget and, almost needless to say, give us a terrific global coup de publicité, in an event which would probably be replayed on Australian television and throughout the world for ever.

You might not get the love from everyone with this work. But the young will always look up to you with awe and even a little respect as you trundle down the streets of Byron in your holiday Shermans.

Finally we promise that, if the Army or police do catch up with you, filling you with bullets, we will give you the most amazing military funeral to which the world's press and television services will, of course, all be invited. We will even build special stands for them – as the IRA did for the world's Press at the funeral of Bobby Sands in Ireland – and put on a special VIP enclosure for your family. There might well be some who would want to dig you up so we just might have to bury you for a while in some obscure sand dune in Syria until it all calms down. It might even be one of the sand dunes that the world is bombing at the moment, trying to kill a terrorist or two. As if. So maybe we'll have to think of a really violent stunt to get the media to come – as they will, they will.

37: Melbourne: City of Dreadful Night

The best place to be to feel the throb and thunder of a great modern city is to take up a position in the middle of one of its main bridges and just watch what surges around you.

Thus it was I stood on the Saint Kilda Bridge over the River Yarra and found myself besieged by the denizens of Melbourne, most noticeably the Chinese who now seem more numerous here than in Shanghai. There were the chortling Italians - there are more of them living here than any of the main towns of Italy - and the Australians themselves, of course, with their bush shorts, tattooed legs and unique cheerful raucousness.

And you then might then spot a slight pasty figure in an old suit shambling along looking miserable. This would be a Pom.

Any number of young girls keep coming with their tiny shorts showing off their endless legs and high heels, all tapping away on their iPhones, and you simply cannot miss the elderly Aussie ladies because they are so fat and they will usually be eating a slice of pizza or a hamburger to keep them going between meals. Young Aussie girls are splendid to look at but it seems, as soon as they have a couple of kids, they just give up and let themselves go straight to the fat dogs.

Next come the backpackers of all nationalities, shouldering packs almost as big as themselves, often bumping into people, usually the drunks who, even this early in the morning, are staggering about in some numbers. There are an unreal number of beggars sitting around on this bridge too, all with plaintive notes written on cardboard about how a few dollars would cheer up their lost lives no end.

The dominance of smart phones seems so complete here as in so many other cities in the world. Everyone seems to be jabbing and poking them and you could only wonder what they were finding to talk about or what they do on the things. I got a clue to that mystery the other night when I was watching a television programme about the work of a Bush hospital. A young girl had come in with her foot badly gashed and in need of cleansing. Oh how she howled and cried in pain when the antiseptic was poured on to her wounds and cleansed. Yet right through the agonising process she kept poking at her mobile in what turned out to be a game. This, you felt, was a real addiction.

I've always loved the genial, subversive eye of Banksy's art and we've done well with his prints in our art gallery in Wales. But I learned the other day that they've found another of his masterpieces on a doorway in a Bristol back street showing two lovers with their arms around one another while at the same time checking their mobile phones over one another's shoulders.

All this bustle is to the accompaniment of Melbourne's trams grinding past with squealing brakes; those heart-stopping relics of another, more glorious, age of public transport. And let's not forget the blue bicycles. Any decent city should have trams and bicycles; they are the first things that should be installed even before the great skyscrapers of steel and coloured glass which loom over you like motionless alien craft. The only trouble with hiring these bicycles is that you need some sort of high-tech degree, including a credit card, to prise one off their stand. Rows of bicycles are always available to anyone who can get through the bureaucratic rules and regulations to pull one out.

***

This was my fourth, albeit brief, visit to this amazing city and I was surprised at how at home I felt on these pavements, even again occasionally spotting myself as a youngster in the merchant navy, living in a cloud of terror, as the young of that age so often do, picking my way through the crowds. I was still on The Canopic.

But one of those first nights here was really scary, perhaps the most scary of my life, and has always stayed in my mind. In short I was caught up in a huge fight on the ship and Melbourne became, for my young mind, The City of Dreadful Night, a place of darkness and punch-ups when I thought I really was about to meet my maker.

We had tied up in Victoria Dock and a new age of international shipping was at its peak here with thousands of immigrants arriving every day, all come to live in the lucky country. The 1956 Olympics had brought Melbourne to the world's attention and the Royal Yacht Britannia was moored here throughout the games.

When I first stepped on to the quay I was, if I may say so, a rather pretty, blue-eyed long-haired youth, who caught the attention of the city's gays who always hung around dock entrances and, in no time at all, I was being followed by a line of about ten of them who just wouldn't take no for an answer. I scooted into the Seamen's Mission to get out of their way and remember sitting with a rather lovely woman explaining to her that, far from sleeping with the men who were following me – and having nothing against gays anyway - I wouldn't at all mind sleeping with her.

But she wasn't having any of that. She was there to cheer up lonely seamen not sleep with them. Well some of the oh-be-joyful would certainly cheer me up, I pointed out, but that line didn't get me anywhere either.

As I later reconstructed events the crew of the Canopic went ashore to catch Melbourne's famous six o'clock swill in the pubs when most seamen had roughly one hour to get as much beer down their throats as they could. This got them well-oiled but that night in question the crew chipped together to buy a few cases of cheap Penfold's sherry which, on top of what they had already drunk, could hit and destroy all their systems like rocket fuel.

They came back to the ship and crowded into the television room where they proceeded to drink the sherry and it all became like that bar in Star Wars. One of the deckhands decided he'd had enough of Australian television, picked up the set and, before anyone knew what was happening, took it out on deck and dropped it in the drink. What followed was bleeding and bloody bedlam and lasted most of the night.

At this point I came walking up the quay after being so cruelly rejected by that woman in the Mission House and the first I saw of all this was the face of a deckhand, covered in blood, staring out of one of the portholes at me. When I got on board it was clear from all the cries and general racket that everyone was fighting everyone else and when the cry went up to get me – as I've said before often enough I was a real pain in the arse then and probably still am - I was quick and lucky enough to get out on to the deck where I spent the night hiding in one of the lifeboats.

***

There was little sign of the old Victoria Dock when Liz and I took a tourist boat out into the harbour the following day and we saw that most of the old quays now had new offices and restaurants built on them. The old cranes had been taken away and all shipping containerised. The old pubs had gone too and they had long abandoned the six o'clock swill. Now you can drink all around the clock and all I recognised from the old days were the black swans moving around on the water, their long necks bent like question marks.

I always get slightly disjointed and even haunted when I go back to the scenes of my mad youth and I certainly had them that day cruising the waters of Victoria Dock. But there was one common thread between then and now which was that I wanted to be a writer then and I was engaged in writing my first violence and perversion-soaked novel on the Canopic.

But four years later came a huge change of tack when, still a young man, I saw my visions from God who explained his supreme anger to me and it was all very different stuff I wrote after that.

Oh yes, my work changed all right after that. As did I.

38: A Welsh nomad loses the plot in Paradise

I stood on the shoreline next to a fir tree watching the sun rise in a huge explosion of angry and threatening red which seemed to make even the distant mountains cower as if they were about to get a good red clip around the ears.

Waders were already up and about on the sand and mud foreshore looking for food in and around the red pools while other larger fowl were cruising the skies in huge shapeless circles like military drones which had lost their navigational equipment. A couple of rabbits came out to graze in the car park.

The red sun turned bright orange, making the whole seascape turn orange too and even the mountains turned the same colour losing their earlier sunburn. Birds cried in strange convoluted sounds, part joyful and part sad, which made no sense, although it all must surely add up to a conversation of sorts, perhaps understood by God alone. The birds dashed about screeching with anxiety as if on urgent errands.

We were in Yanakie, a small ragged village at the entrance to Wilsons Promontory on the southernmost tip of mainland Australia. I adored it here. Everywhere you looked you got intimations of Paradise and this beauty was so penetrating and subversive you just wanted to run around like a mad thing shouting out the good news.

A large lizard walked across the front of our parked Winnebago, his hooded eyes alive with readiness, possibly on the lookout for some hungry bird who might swoop down and eat him. All sorts of birds here would doubtless love to eat a fat lizard, but even so this lizard didn't seem to be in any hurry to get where he was going although there was a certain grim determination in his stride, his little shoulders rising up and down, as if he were a prize fighter on his way to whacking the champion of the world senseless.

The one trouble with this place was that it was freezing cold particularly in the middle of the night, and that was because of the frequent winds, fresh in off the ocean, which blew hard. These winds created their own sound in the trees, almost exactly like a swelling sea, which is rather odd as the sea itself was so still and flat this morning. Perhaps they took it in turns. The noise in the trees certainly seemed to scare the birds which kept fluttering up out of the woodland rooftops shrieking with dismay, doubtless feeling the same cold lash of those fresh sea winds too.

At four thirty in the afternoon, always on the dot, another gang of birds came from somewhere to roost in the fir trees where we were parked. These were galahs - cockatoos with pink heads and vast pink underbellies - who all shouted at one another for twenty minutes or so before going out on to the sands where about a hundred of them suddenly shut up and scratched around looking for something to eat.

The dark pink of these galahs suggested they might even have just been in some long bloody fight and reminded me of one of my favourite stories about how the robin got his red breast. He had been around at the time of the Crucifixion, it seemed, and there was one thorn in the crown which had been causing Jesus real pain so he asked the robin to pull it out. As the robin did so he caught a splash of blood over his breast and it stayed there ever since. "I got my red breast because I was there when Jesus died."

Here in Yanakie I had quite forgotten about my Grey Nomads who seemed to have disappeared from my life along with the sun and warmth. Typical Grey Nomad behaviour that. Expose them to a gust of wind or rain and they're gone.

But then I bumped into one in a car park and he was Welsh too. I was first attracted to him by his Welsh accent, and discovered that he was originally from Newport in South Wales, a slaughterhouse man and butcher by trade. He had come to Australia with his wife and had two children who had then gone on to give him numerous grandchildren, their photographs festooning the walls of his comfortable caravan.

They'd been real Grey Nomads, without any real home, for two years now. While the other nomads liked to go north for the sun these two preferred to stay south because it was cooler. His health was terrible though – at 69 he had just about every illness going – and he had to have an injection for some kind of cancer every month at a hospital no matter where he was. Aussie health care is fantastic.

We chatted happily for nearly an hour mostly about butchery and his health, while his wife made the tea, when, apropos of nothing, he said he was in the butchery business only for a few years before becoming an Anglican minister – and later a full-time chaplain in various prisons. But now he had given all that up. He was no longer a believer.

You what? You've been a minister all your life and there you are riddled with cancer and you've given it all up? It was all scarcely credible. You'd have thought that at this stage in his tricky proceedings he'd have kept up a little fire insurance or something. He didn't even pray any more.

"Prison life was all right. You always knew where you were with the old lags. But I just couldn't keep dealing with people who always expected me to do everything for them."

I told him I was a believer which seemed to come as a genuine surprise to him. People rarely guess that about me unless I tell them but he appeared less interested in what I believed and became still gloomier when I told him that God had had a word with me about it all and dragooned me, much against my will, into becoming one of his extremely reluctant prophets.

"Oh I just can't believe in all that stuff," he said with a dismissive wave of his hand. "I'm not into that at all."

So I sat gazing at a man who suddenly seemed to be just sitting there in a shroud of darkness and ashes. He was clearly a good man who'd tried to live a life of love but somehow or other he'd become a sort of Graham Greene whisky priest who had dug one big hole for himself out here in the Bush.

Another disappointed romantic, I thought, rather like most of the clerical heroes of Greene's novels. But, after such a life would God actually reach out to him at the end and haul him back up? I just don't know; I didn't have the faintest clue.

But then in spiritual matters, I have often found, you just never know what's coming around the bend. All I know is that God can show you a lost priest one minute and the next you are out here on Wilsons Promontory meeting wombats on the road and red parrots swirling in the skies and seeing mountains which turn from red to yellow first thing in the morning. Yes, these were all arguments for belief in a divine creator, I was sure and you really did want to run around shouting out the good news.

Well, I did anyway.

39: Jacko's Monkey in Reincarnation Shock

I really do dislike almost everything about the modern media but, as I have intimated earlier in this book – or perhaps everywhere in this book - I fear there's still a bit of the old hack in me struggling to get out particularly if someone dangles the juicy bone of a good story in front of me.

This happened in Coral Bay earlier this year, I'm sorry to report, when I learned that a blowfish had bitten off some poor woman's little toe and I also have to admit to a certain satisfaction and even excitement when a little boy was heartbroken after presumably the same fish bit a big hole in one of his flippers. That blowfish had clearly not had his fill with that woman's toe and had come back for a chunk of rubber to finish off its lunch.

Anyway this was a real story – and what's more it even turned out to be true as I had interviewed everyone concerned – and I was in full hack heaven when the owner of the shell shop stood in front of me as I wielded my Biro and notebook under his nose, and kept lying through his teeth saying that a blowfish like this only turned up once in a lifetime and he could never recollect anything like this happening to tourist toes before. Even as he was saying this the park ranger and owner of the site had been discussing whether to put up a sign on the beach warning of these blowfish. Once in a lifetime eh?

So when I was told the story of Tom the Killer Whale who had been operating in the sea just off the town of Eden on the south coast I was up and running again waving my Biro and notebook in the air.

There was a long purple cloud with small knobs on it – oh yes, there was - stretching across a sunshine sky with the distant mountain of Imlay and its sharp tip - as if it had just been put through a giant pencil sharpener - staring down at us as we sputtered out of Eden harbour into the Tasman Sea accompanied by a couple of hopeful pelicans. We had been staying on a campsite called, inevitably, the Garden of Eden, and our hunt had begun on a small charter fishing boat, the Connemara.

I can't remember who first told me about Tom but his story had been playing on my mind for some time. He was clearly something of a superhero in the whale world having performed numerous acts to help the whalers of Eden, building up the whaling industry here almost single-handedly before whaling was banned in the 1970s. Now whales are almost everywhere here in Twofold Bay, in season, and although we had missed the end of the season by a day, we were still guaranteed to see some sort of whale for our eighty dollars or get a full refund.

No whale came with such a glorious back story as Tom's who, with his gang of about twenty other killer whales such as Big Jack, Hooky, Humpy and Fatty, would hang around the entrance to this bay and herd passing baleen whales right into the harbour and on to the harpoons of the waiting whalers who all became rich and successful because of Tom and his gang; a sort of outsize and slippery Ned Kelly of the deep.

Tom and his friends also protected the whalers from shark attacks or "hop-tailed" to alert them to a pod of baleens that might just be going past. Tom was also a "bit of a lad" who would grab a line from one of the whaling boats and take it on a wild ride out in the bay just for the joy of it, earning him the nickname of Tom Tug. Another of the killer whales was said to have rescued a drowning whaler and carried him back to his ship. As a reward for this co-operation the whalers allowed the killers the baleen tongues, lips and flippers which the killers really loved above all else.

The more I learned about these killers the more I disbelieved it. These stories all smelled of myth and exaggeration, I thought gloomily as I stared out at a sea, empty of everything but sunlight. I had been a journalist for many years beginning with the Western Mail in Wales and then on the Sunday Times, the Sunday Telegraph and the Observer, where I had built something of an undeserved reputation for writing stories based on very little, but even I couldn't see how this Tom the Killer Whale guff could add up to anything other than the smallest hill of sprats unless I happened to land a job on the Daily Star which once ran my favourite phoney headline which went: Jacko's Monkey in Re-incarnation Shock. It seems to me you can write anything at all if you work for the Daily Star.

I was also a bit sceptical, to put it mildly, on the issue of the killers herding the baleens into the harbour and all those miraculous rescues. I remembered the stories I picked up when I did a number of pilgrimages throughout Europe in recent years, particularly the one on the road to Compostela where almost every church had their own chickens and goats which could cure everything - even death. One story told of a roasted cock which, having been cooked, stood up on the dining table and began to crow. Allegedly.

All this to beef up the pilgrim trade as these stories about killer whales had doubtless been invented to beef up the tourist trade here.

They had even got their own miracle cure here in the town of Eden when they would get a carcass of a dead whale and drill a big hole in its side. Three semi-naked people would climb into this hole and stay there for up to two hours. Apart from making them stink for weeks this "treatment" was said to cure rheumatism and even arthritis.

And then my story about Tom the killer whale received a killer blow when I learned that Tom had in fact died on September 13, 1930 and his carcass had been found washed up in a local bay by a whaler out walking his dog. Furthermore they hadn't seen a killer whale out these ways for years although they were still very hopeful of tracking down a few humpbacks for us today.

But all of us on the charter out of Eden went into fantastic leaps of joy when about two hundred dolphins emerged all around us as we puttered on. Our skipper said he could never remember so many dolphins turning up at the same time as they kept dancing around us like a huge gang of demented Cardiff City football supporters who had just reached the top of the Premiership for the first time in its long suffering history. Believe me on this: I have followed Cardiff City all my life and can only remember five minutes of happiness during all that time. I too would dance forever if they topped the Premiership but that's never going to happen. Ever.

The Connemara was so small I could stretch out on the front deck of the prow and practically get my hands into the water as the dolphins came dancing all around, sending water splashing all over my face as they leaped into the air and dived straight down again into the waves. And these boys could swim – no doubt about that – shooting just beneath the water with the speed of bullets before leaping out just ahead of the boat and my outstretched hands while the boat was doing a pretty fast lick too.

This play went on for about half an hour – one of the most joyous half hours of my life – and by now I had forgotten, and certainly ceased to care, why we had sailed out here in the first place. But then we saw a sight so moving we all stood up on the boat and cheered.

At first there was a tall dorsal fin amid a lot of disturbed foam and this huge, shiny, black mass of blubber came rising up out of the water and we marvelled at the whole body of the humpback as it rose up in front of us and sank downwards, with just its outsize tail fin left, farewelling us. Hang around, the tail said, and I'll be back up again in about ten minutes. Or maybe it didn't. It was really hard to tell what it was saying with all the racket going on in our boat. Those not actually still shouting were drying their eyes of tears, brought on by the sheer gobsmacking wonder of what we had just seen.

So it was a great day for everyone out in Twofold Bay and we all hugged the skipper at the end of it for doing us proud. But, believe it or not, I did actually catch up with Tom the Killer Whale later that day. The encounter wasn't in the sea, alas, but in the local museum where his skeleton was mounted on wires. I gave his leg a congratulatory pat and wondered if I might get a story out of him after all.

And then I'm sure he muttered through his broken teeth: Oh just make it up. When did you lot ever worry about the truth anyway?

Well I think he said that. Or perhaps he didn't.

40: How Australia was flogged into the Modern World

We have just woken up on the spot where the famed convicts of Australia first opened up the wilderness of the Bush in 1820 and built a village in Coolangatta, the first ever outside the cities in the whole of this wondrous land.

There are no plaques or monuments here and you even have to look quite hard for clues to how and why this place was first built. We forsook the Winnebago and took the stable suite where they have retained the original stable doors and rafters. There are also the remnants of the original horse stalls in the living room but otherwise it could be a suite in any modern hotel with a microwave, television and a bath so big you needed to be a good swimmer or you could easily have drowned in it.

This village now has some twenty dwellings, with a restaurant in the old community centre, and sits on top of a hill overlooking a creek up which those first convicts would have sailed in from Sydney. About 100 of them climbed that hill in their clanking manacles and leg irons and came out on to this clearing where they dug the first footings of this village and were flogged mercilessly if they stepped out of line.

Archives tell us there really couldn't have been a worse life for these poor, luckless souls who had been yanked out of their homes in some poor London slum, transported across the world and welcomed by hostile Aborigines who occasionally threw spears at them or even ate them. When the convicts were flogged, often for trivial reasons, the skin was taken clean off the bones of their backs and the flogger might then have to start on their legs. The other convicts were forced to witness these psychopathic assaults with flecks of blood often striking their eyes if the wind was blowing in a certain direction.

The man who led the first group here was Alexander Berry, another of those bug-eyed Scots for whom nothing was impossible. He began as a liberal on flogging, according to Robert Hughes, in his seminal work Fatal Shore, but ended up calling for more leg irons and cat o'nine tails. "Ungrateful and irredeemable profligates who have been made more comfortable than at any time in their lives," Berry later moaned about his convicts.

He first landed in Sydney in 1808 and ended up owning 40,000 acres by 1873. He died at the age of 102 and the only ports bigger than nearby Shoalhaven at that time were Sydney, Newcastle and Wollongong. Indeed Berry's whole life stretched over the history of transportation and it weirded us out a bit knowing we had just been sleeping next to his bedroom, now reduced to one plastered wall after the rest of the house was burned down in suspicious circumstances, perhaps by a convict who objected to being flogged black and blue. Outside his bedroom was a rich blue bed of fragrant agapanthus. These lovely flowers flourish everywhere like heavenly carpets in this part of the world.

In a recent renovation old newspapers, used at the time as wallpaper, were stripped off the walls. One report in 1852 told of the loss of a pocket book containing two £5 notes and one £1 note which left the former owner of the money a poor man with not a shilling to his name. Pritchard's Authentic Steel Pills were claimed to cure everything and the clipper Galatea was up for sale.

After Berry's death the pastoral elite here moved away from flogging to keep law 'n' order. One man told the Committee of Transportation it was "best when a man behaves well, where possible, to make him forget he is a convict". Another said, "The belly is far more vulnerable and sensitive than the back. Use the carrot not the whip. Stay clear of the courts because constant appeals to the power of higher authorities will ultimately diminish your own power. Become paternal and the men will come to trust you out of respect and love for you rather than live in fear of another bloody beating."

The restaurant now has a Convict Banquet every Saturday night and all around are carefully manicured lines of vineyards. Perhaps inevitably there is also that most Scottish of creations, a golf course.

The story of transportation is one of the most compelling I know with its cruel and savage beginnings, often in the fetid slums of London, a journey like no other across the world and a truly wonderful ending: nothing less than the creation of the whole of Australia. And what a creation Australia is, built on a scaffolding of human endeavour and sheer fabulousness. The convicts didn't actually do it all, of course, but they certainly got it going. In tiny villages such as this Australia got on her way.

***

The Grey Nomads have now gone completely AWOL from our lives and we were surprised by how much we missed them and their help and friendliness. Indeed this loss was reinforced when we pulled into Kiama for a few nights on our way back to Sydney and even though the site had the most perfect setting right on a sandy beach, guarding a whiffling sea, we found the place a bit of a nightmare in which no one spoke to us at all, not even the ritual g'day.

The holidaymakers here were generally young with lots of kids and we couldn't even establish eye contact with any of them. They came in large groups of friends who partied noisily until late and would put on their radios with the latest hits at full blast, starting first thing in the morning. You would never catch a Grey Nomad doing that; they had too much respect for others and neither would they have allowed their dogs to keep barking morning, noon and night either.

There was also a group of youngsters who gathered on the beach all day and just kept making a racket and doing daft stuff.

One of the real features of Australian life, I now understand, is that the younger you are the more unpleasant you can be, particularly when you are in a gang. Older young men with tattooed muscles and long hair bleached blonde by the sun don't have much to say either.

With all this mind we decided on a change of tack to while away the month or so before our planned Christmas in Manly so we registered with Happy House Sitters on the net – look, that's what they call themselves - and in no time at all received an invitation to come to a house in the Blue Mountains where the owners were going on a holiday and our duties would be to baby-sit two dogs, a dozen or so chickens and a lizard.

This break from the road would all clearly give us a new dimension on Australia and, more crucially, it would also surely be good fun. It's not every day you get to look after a lizard: I did hope he wouldn't bite.

41: The Bald Cat with a Hole in its Forehead

The Blue Mountains are an enormous gathering of sandstone escarpments and gorges not far from Sydney, smothered with huge eucalypt forests which shiver continuously with the chatterings of cicadas and winds talking to the leaves. They are called blue because that's what they are, something to do with eucalyptus oil in the air meeting up with the sunlight. It all rises up over you like an enormous blue bruise, settling across the deep valleys and high flat cliff faces.

The best part of these mountains are the great waterfalls which spew over the tops of the cliffs, forever trumpeting the triumphant news of the eternal marriage between water and gravity.

We stayed in Blackheath as we waited to start our first house-sitting gig, a lovely town which stank of money and good manners with shops which were perfect in every random detail. We loved it here and could have easily have wandered into one of the houses for sale, bought it and settled down and finally died surrounded by friendship and happiness. Everyone we met was lovely.

The campsite was marvellously serene - after they managed to evict a gang of bogans who wanted to party all night - although we were awoken there every morning by a family of birds who seemed to be involved in an endless mass brawl which just went on and on. It turned out to be a family of magpies who were trying to get their babies to fledge and look after themselves. But this meant that the chicks would have to find their own food which they didn't like at all. So the row was between the parents telling the kids they had to get their own food and their kids following them around determinedly yelling that they should shape up to their parental responsibilities and get it for them.

We were a bit nervous about taking up our first house sitting job in nearby Wentworth Falls which involved looking after two enormous chocolate labradors, Noah and Millie, a load of chickens and Lemmy the Lizard. Our confidence wasn't much improved when we were having breakfast in a local café before going to the house for the first time, and a young chemist sitting at our table learned what we were about to do.

Oh yes, he said, he used to do pet sitting. He had a call from a woman asking him to look after a cat for a month. She even offered to pay him well, which is not normal practice for this kind of work, and as he was desperate for money at the time and hated the student digs where he lived he took it on. When he got there he found that the cat in question was a "completely bald testicle", an Ukrainian Levkoy, with a large hole in his forehead. And this hole was something of a problem.

The woman explained that what she wanted him to do – twice a day – was to put on a plastic glove and put his finger in a jar of special ointment and insert it into the hole. This caused the cat some pain but it had learned that it felt a good deal better in the end so it didn't run away when it was time for the plastic finger. He added that everything worked out fine and he even became good friends with the cat.

Cripes! I wasn't at all sure I could do anything like that no matter how broke I was and when I later told a girl this story in a party in Sydney she disappeared into the toilet in a state of shock for a good half hour and never spoke to me again.

But our job in Wentworth Falls turned out fine – all the animals had completely normal foreheads with no holes in them and the only work, if it could be called that, was keeping the labradors fed because they were hungry all the time and, when they weren't being fed, they kept trying to lick you to death. The chickens were pretty well-behaved too, each dutifully laying an egg every morning which soon made me sick of eggs. Chickens are so stupid: you can never get any sense out of them.

Liz said she was happy to look after the dogs and chickens leaving me with Lemmy the Lizard. All I had to do was feed him with live crickets which I was sure would be a breeze - although I was soon to learn otherwise.

Lemmy was an Eastern Water Dragon, about a foot long with a long tail and white and green scales. He spent his time sitting motionless on the heated rock in his aquarium in the dining room and I soon saw that not only the dogs watched every morsel I put in my mouth closely but Lemmy did too, his beady eyes swivelling from side to side and taking in my every move and chew.

A small disaster happened when I first tried to feed Lemmy his crickets since all the crickets took it as an opportunity to jump for their freedom as soon as I opened their box, bouncing all over the dining table and floor with me desperately trying to recapture them (I only got about half). Then I had an even bigger problem when I opened the lid of the aquarium to pop in a cricket or two which Lemmy took as a cue to try and make a break for it. I hadn't thought he could move at all but he could, faster than greased lightning. Luckily, as he shot upwards, propelled by his long, sinewy legs, I just about managed to jam the lid back down on his head.

I was shaking badly now; I really didn't want my first house sitting job marred by the loss of the family lizard although I would have happily and quickly dropped him in a local pond had he been mine.

When it came to eating, Lemmy could scoff for Sydney. Slugs, snails, crickets … you name it, he swallowed them whole without so much as a token chew. Lizards will eat anything that moves, it soon became clear, and I later learned that lizards will even attack and rob streams of ants, stealing their food as they try to carry it home to their nests.

But now I didn't even dare open his lid except once, as an experiment, I put his crickets inside a Woolworth's plastic bag with the intention of shaking them out when he was elsewhere in the aquarium. But I was in trouble again when he hurdled the length of the aquarium, grabbing hold of the bag with his sharp talons and refusing to let go. He swung around and around like a regular little Tarzan and it took me a good ten minutes to shake him off back into his pool.

Lizards are not as thick as they look and even have something of a brain, one of my readers told me later and indeed she had three herself, one of whom followed her around her house all day.

***

Then came another problem: I had run out of crickets, with half having been eaten by Lemmy and the other half out on the lam in the Blue Mountains. What to do? I was sitting watching television one night when a big bug flew past me and I managed to jump up, catch it and feed it to Lemmy who, as usual, swallowed it whole. This became the pattern of the evenings and I spent more time in the living room scanning the air for Lemmy food than reading or watching television.

One night I was sitting on the toilet and was appalled to see a giant cockroach on top of my bar of soap on the washbasin. I decided not to chase it largely because I had found they are too fast for me. Yet the following day I was back in the bathroom and found this same cockroach preening himself on my toothbrush. Right, that was it. I got a rolled-up copy of the Australian newspaper and running faster than a rocket with daps on I gave him a good clonk which concussed him while also scattering my toiletries all over the bathroom floor.

Liz came in wondering what all the shouting and swearing was about and suggested I feed the unconscious cockroach to Lemmy. But would he like it? Oh sure he'd like it all right. That lizard likes everything.

It was one extremely happy Eastern Water Dragon who swallowed the cockroach whole and just sat there on his stone with all those little cockroach legs waving and squirming as they poked out of the sides of his fat greedy red lips.

This pantomime went on for two weeks and I was pretty relieved but said nothing when the owners returned. There was a bittersweet end to this story, though. I was watching Sir David Attenborough talking about lizards on television on our last night there and he said: "The one thing about lizards is they can keep going for weeks without needing any food."

42: City Wrapped in a Cocoon of Violence

It was like greeting a much-loved friend we hadn't seen for years when Mrs Sat Nav took us back into Sydney, almost a year after she had taken us out. There were the central huddled mass of skyscrapers, the big coathanger bridge and all those huge sunglazed coves with small yachts bobbing about on the water looking expensive. Our hearts also always rose a couple of points when we clapped our eyes on the Opera House, just sitting there on her promontory, as improbably as the back ends of a couple of excited lobsters about to mate, and where we had sat through that wonderful concert by Neil Finn when we first arrived here.

Mrs Sat Nav had taken us everywhere throughout Australia and you sometimes hoped she might also get excited at moments like this. But she never did. Everything is calm and devoid of emotion in Sat Nav world - even when we have taken the wrong turning - although it was the strangest weather for our Sydney return with thunder rumbling quietly and the clouds turning into the oddest shapes which might mean something in meteorological circles but we didn't know what.

We drove to Manly where we were again staying with our youngest son Nathan and his partner Sally. A few days later we took the ferry to Circular Quay when, after a few false starts, the promised storm broke, landing with huge flashes of lightning ripping into the city's dark skyline, followed by terrifying cracks of thunder and pouring rain.

I've decided I am going to add up the ways in which so much violence is now sluicing through this city's veins. It is something I've been thinking of doing for a long time since I believe it might even tell a truth behind this city's amazing beauty and elegance, perhaps helping you to understand why she is soon going to stumble and fall. Many are going to hate what I am about to write – most people who have ever stayed in this city love it unreservedly - but I hope they do at least read, and think about, what I have to say first. And I hope they always keep in mind that we too are madly in love with Australia in general and Sydney in particular and they take this as a warning made with love and not a judgment in wrath.

The cinema is popular here and Brad Pitt's new one, Fury, is showing in the Auburn. This film keeps giving you terrible glimpses, one critic wrote: tank tracks rolling over a dead body half-buried in mud, an elderly woman cutting meat off a dead horse, a woman in a wedding dress surrounded by lots of refugees. "An unrelentingly violent depiction of war," wrote another critic. "Bayonets in the eye, bullets in the back, limbs blown apart, corpses and human parts sprayed everywhere."

Brad himself turned in a good, clever performance though, even managing some subtlety in the mayhem all around.

The new Hunger Games: Mockingjay - Part 1, had also opened in the Bankstown cinema. It contains a lot of graphic violence and early in the story people, with bags over their heads, are executed at point-blank range or beheaded, a timely reminder of what our terrorists are now doing in the Middle East and elsewhere - in case we need reminding.

Another popular and well-reviewed film, Gone Girl, is showing in the Bondi Junction cinema. This also has many graphic and prolonged scenes of murder including one in a bed with a naked woman repeatedly stabbing a naked man, with the sheer terror of the stabbings ramped up to fever pitch by loud slashes of orchestral music. This scene makes the original Psycho stabbing scene look as harmless as a walk to a drugstore to buy some headache pills which you really will need after watching it.

Television news runs on the main channels all day. There are bits and pieces about health or traffic jams but the main thrust of all this frantic activity is the obsessional search for violence – any violence. Today they are yet again featuring the discovery of a dead baby in a drain a few days ago by a couple of children playing on a Sydney beach. Police are gathered where the body was discovered and news desks take the opportunity to show yet again footage of the drain down which the baby had been dumped. We may have been shown the inside of this drain dozens of times. They also like to hark back to older, similar stories while doing this and showing again where other dead babies were found.

This is clearly these news desks' way of keeping up their violence ratio. The VR they call it in the business. Or they also talk about the Bang Bang factor. They also keep showing – on the flimsiest of pretexts – that aeroplane crashing into that New York skyscraper on September 11.

Australian television has also plumbed new depths in inanity with a new reality show, Go Back to Where You Came From which takes fame-hungry morons to various danger-spots of the world so they can experience what it's like to be a refugee.

The next day the Sydney news featured terrorists shooting more men for not being Muslims in Kenya. The news showed us the bodies stretched out in lines on the dust and this was clearly deemed to be a cue to show yet again the Nairobi footage when the Boko Haram thugs were running around shooting shoppers in a supermarket there about a year ago. Television news desks seem to have a real fondness for that bit of footage, particularly the bit of the children cowering behind display cabinets in the supermarket.

Elsewhere today there's been a bit of a siege in Melbourne, which doesn't really look much like a siege, with a man in his boxer shorts being led away by the police. Another man has been arrested for a fatal shooting in WA and yet another arrested for threatening an embassy official. A yoga teacher is being tried for the murder of a young girl.

Aha, here's some live footage of a young girl allegedly beaten by the police with truncheons for resisting arrest. The cameras make a full and minute examination of the bruises on her fat, bare legs which she shows off proudly in full like a model advertising tights. We see these bruises in close-up again and again throughout the week until they fade away.

Television news editors here love any kind of injury which is always good for a minute or two. A while ago a rugby footballer had suffered a black eye and we were daily treated to close-ups of said eye until, by the following Friday, it had got better. If all these victims of the most minor assaults were on repeat fees they would make a fortune.

Yikes. Someone had sent in mobile footage of a drunken fight in Kings Cross. We are shown it three or four times throughout the evening in case we missed the wild punches the first time. But it's only yet another a drunken fight in Kings Cross and none of the punches seem to connect either so no black eyes to keep drooling over there.

What these news services love, of course, almost more than anything else, is the slightest whiff of terrorist activity on which they will leap as a starving dog on a juicy bone. Just lately there have been police raids in Sydney and the television cameras are always there right next to the cops as they go crashing through the suspects' doors. The police never find much – a hammer perhaps or a ceremonial sword – and the local police chief is always interviewed after the raid when he usually says that, in such times, you can never be too careful.

In such times? And careful of what exactly?

When you watch television news on any one night you would assume that every Sydney street is on a war footing. There is no truth in this coverage and, in any discussion about the meaning of reality and its relationship to truth, these news bulletins, together with the violent films we have been talking about, are all lies.

Politicians love to get involved too. Premier Tony Abbott always had something to say about terrorism before his party ousted him as had defence secretary Julie Bishop, a real media tart if ever there was one, photographed the other night reading her official papers in bed in her jimjams. She didn't say anything but had allowed the cameras into her bedroom to record her in bed reading her papers.

So many of these Aussie politicians seem to nurture fantasies of global power and are hungry for any kind of world coverage. The name of the game is bigging yourself up, I guess, and they all appear to want Australia to have a place on the world stage and be part of the same great world drama.

None of what I am listing here may come to you as any sort of surprise but, when you put it all together, it might enable you to understand the scale and nature of this attack on this city by its media. It is daily, hourly and intense and issues out of a media which is rubbish and keeps putting out rubbish. And not harmless rubbish either but mind-deadening, spirit-chilling rubbish which has a lot to do with Rupert Murdoch and his gang who set the tone and pace of most media activity in this part of the world.

The local television services do make other programmes when they are not actually scrabbling in the gutters looking for blood or bodies. The main features are cookery and house makeover programmes which regularly top the charts sometimes taking up all the top ten places.

The dark shadow of censorship doesn't fall over any part of my thoughts although what I am trying to show here is how far this romantic evil stretches and how deep it goes. It is almost everywhere flooding our minds with the purest evil and only God himself will know what terrible monsters this evil will finally hatch.

***

The thunder and rain eased as suddenly as it had started and we got on a bus which took us through the crowded, sweltering Sydney streets, everywhere humming with banners proclaiming the coming Christmas. There was a real festive music in these streets and a charabanc swept past us. Then the Christmas music stopped for me. Absolutely stopped. A huge poster on the side of the bus was advertising the new Black Ops video game, another poster on another bus was welcoming the new Assassin's Creed game and another poster featured our old friend Grand Theft Auto, possibly the most violent and certainly sickest game ever devised for the entertainment of our lost and betrayed youth.

When one American lawyer, Jack Thompson, described Grand Theft Auto as the gravest attack on our children since polio he did not go far enough. This thing is the biggest attack on children ever mounted, bigger even than all the famines and diseases put together, since this game attacks all those who play it: where children live, breathe and grow – in their ideas; in what they become and go on to do. For this is no mere game to play and put aside but an activity often lasting many hours in which you actually become the thug and criminal yourself, in which you take out people who get in your way, murder passers-by and even rape women. You can even murder policemen and be rewarded for doing so.

We are all no more than our ideas about ourselves and the world is no more than the sum of our ideas about it. Our ideas control everything we do and, if those ideas are poisoned at a very young age - as I was with the garbage I started my own life with - many of our children can really look forward to nothing at all, except perhaps a long life on a wooden bed in a prison cell together with a long view of the world behind prison bars.

I have written extensively in my books about the mass killings that are currently plaguing our schools, especially in America, and this Black Ops video game has featured in many. Anders Breivik played the game almost non-stop for a year to prepare himself for his slaughter of those 66 youngsters in Oslo in 2011.

Another invincible romantic, Breivik was always looking to the media to make him famous and, when the police wanted to photograph him after he was arrested, he protested that they really should use the photo-shopped studio images he had taken of himself and posted online. Wanting to look his best after his massacre this "Christian crusader" needed to show himself in makeup and in muscular poses, wearing military uniform covered with medals. The words "Marxist Hunter" were stitched on his sleeve.

The youth who slaughtered the kids in a school in Sandy Hook, Connecticut, in December 2012, killing 20 children and six staff members, also played the Black Ops game obsessively. Since then there have been 87 school shootings in America - with the figures rising almost every week - and everyone is still missing the point by shouting about gun control. Look at your entertainment, Americans.

The new Black Ops, Call of Duty – along with the others – was given an absolutely rapturous review in Rupert Murdoch's Australian here in Sydney in a round-up of all the new Christmas video releases. "Call of Duty is an intense and amazingly rendered game with drones to manipulate, exo-suits to float in the air and an arsenal of high tech weapons to kill at will," the reviewer drooled.

What he of all people should understand – particularly as a reviewer and a father - is that such games deliver images and ideas that the immature and downright stupid in our midst absorb and act upon. But oh no. Such reviewers hardly ever type a critical word.

***

You would never accuse newspapers of having the same pernicious influence as video games although Rupert Murdoch's bordello of television companies and newspapers is clearly responsible for much of the poisoning publicity in which the reptiles of ISIS are spawned and fattened here in Australia and elsewhere in the world, giving them bigger presences, stages and voices with which they can frighten everyone with their beheadings and other outrages.

Murdoch's Australian is a strange newspaper, largely written by right-wing ideologues who all seem obsessed by themselves and their ideas, often writing comment pieces which masquerade as news and generally reflect the mental thuggery of their editor.

These hacks are forever bullying Canberra politicians, holding them up or dragging them down, often with the help of the most vicious leader columns that take no prisoners. They are all Rupert's barking dogs, very touchy too particularly about any accusation they are controlled by Rupert on Skype. But he is always telling them what to do. That's the way he is made and a couple of months ago he gave an incomprehensible speech about wealth creation which the Australian newspaper turned into a front page lead. The following day's front page lead was full of praise for the same speech by various political and industrial leaders including one who announced he "danced with joy" when he read the speech. Danced with joy!

Almost everyone here watches television which has become a key part of the national conversation. Australians watch it on an average of 97 hours a month or for more than three hours a day. And let us never forget that every body of research, more than 120 of them, both in the UK and America, has found a link between violence on screen and social violence. Every single one of them!

***

European television drama companies have also made a large contribution to this black cloud of murder and violence now hanging so thickly over Sydney and indeed over almost all the major cities of the world. They have produced highly praised television dramas which portray, with some style, whole gangs of shuffling killers who, with the Marquis de Sade in one pocket and Stieg Larsson in the other, act out their bloodthirsty narratives as they murder women in long drawn-out scenes shot in semi-darkness, accompanied by a lot of huffing and panting which makes you feel sick right from the beginning of each interminable scene and even sicker as it gets to the end.

Needless to say the television critics often cheer this romantic gangrene to the echo. No one I'm aware of told us we were now watching serialised terrorism in which terrorists and dramatists both appear to have the same aim which is to incite the stupid to spread violence in the streets and their own lives. Television has no token age rules either unlike the cinema – although they do pay lip service to it often by offering some kind of warning which, I've often thought, actually promotes what they are allegedly warning about – but we should remember the killing is usually well under way by 8pm on Sydney television anyway and doesn't let up all night.

In the real world 15 people were shot in the streets of Sydney, in a wave of assassinations and drive-bys, in just the *last month* of 2014.

The Killing was perhaps the biggest of these series promoting murder, in which the Danes committed twenty hours of television to a plot propped up by murder. This was followed by others in a similar style including The Bridge which opened with two body parts set on either side of the centre of a bridge joining two European countries. There was also Broadchurch from the UK with much the same, hugely praised by all the critics who should have known better, and garlanded with awards everywhere it was shown.

Then we had the wretched The Fall in which a Belfast serial killer is a family man and grief counsellor who fantasises about tying up, torturing and killing his daughter's Barbie dolls. The problem – for him, us and indeed the already sorry image of Belfast – is that he then goes off into the night and does much the same by torturing, raping and killing real women in scenes almost unbearable in their prolonged and sadistic cruelty.

I was out of the country for The Missing, which was a chip off the same block I heard, although the surprise for me was seeing Happy Valley on Australian television, a BBC production set in a sleepy town in Yorkshire, which was far from happy and, again in scenes which were pure violent pornography, we saw people kidnapped, blindfolded and tortured while we got the sweet Sarah Lancashire actually sticking the boot into someone lying on the street at least a dozen times. Sarah Lancashire!

So what we have in plain sight here are boats and ships and even passenger liners are all set adrift on the great seas of the world and all packed to the gunwhales with romantic gangrene, this philosophical poison which they unload into the living rooms of the world soaking everything with blood as zombies fight one another knee-deep in the afterbirth of a million back street abortions. These ships travel anywhere and everywhere, disgorging their violent narratives throughout our culture which are busily gripping the imaginations of our sick and stupid to join in the killing while no one anywhere seems to understand why they are doing it.

The one thing we now know for certain is that a lot more of this trash, which outrages all the laws of imitative form, will be speeding to Australia and add to the shameful darkness which is now spreading its black evil wings all over the face of the Australian sun. No wonder God's heart is breaking, no wonder he's looking on in pure despair as all these romantic, violent narratives are taking hold everywhere. He knows far better than anyone how far this death toll is going to rise before someone, somewhere, screams for all these murders to stop *and gets listened to.*

***

As we continued travelling around Sydney that day I could not help giving a wry smile when I noticed a large white cross painted on the side of a building next to the Harbour Bridge. For those with eyes to see it seemed so at odds with all those emblems of media evil lurking all around us; this powerful symbol of hope and redemption, what the Welsh poet RS Thomas once called the Untenanted Cross, now surely waiting for a new tenant in this age which is clearly ruled over by a Man of Lawlessness.

So who is the Man of Lawlessness? Well we can occasionally spot clues to his identity when we find him lurking in the depths of the Bible. First we understand that he has a magnetic personality and is able to control politicians and even the very elect of God. He will take over the whole world and every home, ruling through error and deception. He will also come dressed in respectability and anxious to serve us. He will even make us laugh.

But our best sighting of him comes in the writings of St Paul, a spirit-filled prophet who was the first man to understand the life and death of Jesus Christ. Paul spent a turbulent life founding and encouraging different churches when he learned that many of its members had become frustrated and unhappy. They had given up work and were eagerly awaiting the Second Coming. But when was it happening? This is a familiar Christian dilemma: caught between the summer lightning of the First Coming and the apocalyptic thunder of the Second.

The Second Coming is referred to 318 times in the 210 chapters of the New Testament. It was Christ's greatest and most repeated promise but Paul told his people to settle down and go back to work because the times weren't right. Before any Second Coming the Man of Lawlessness, a Satanic parody of the true Messiah and a great threat to society, must come first. This being will oppose Christ and everything holy. He will reign with all the "powers and miracles of the lie" but, when the time is right, he will be ruthlessly exposed in his own season. Only then can we look forward to the return of our Man of Sorrows.

Whatever happens next – and a lot will happen – we should understand we have all now entered the long-promised season of the Man of Lawlessness who is the mind of the modern media: the violence-loving, scandal-dealing, vampire-breeding, confidence-sapping, blasphemy-preaching, riot-provoking, terrorist-supporting perversion-embracing, apocalypse-promoting, compulsively lying, pornography adoring, politically controlling mind of the modern media which is so full of deception and lies it even fools those who work for it.

Over the years there have been any number of candidates put forward for the role of the Man of Lawlessness, ranging from Nero to Judas Iscariot, the rotten emperors of Rome, Luther, Calvin and even Hitler. But even all herded together we can be sure that they could not even hold up a candle to the all-destroying sun of the modern media which has put every single one of us in its sights.

Look what we've managed to create today: right before your very eyes.

43: Who Breaks a Butterfly on a Wheel?

I have never understood the writing process; for me the very act is full of strangeness, unpredictability and pure unintelligibility. Words and ideas seem to come together for no reason and my most creative time will come at the moment I awake in the morning and lie there with ideas just stumbling into my mind like drunks trying to find their way home but then collapsing in a coma on the floor of my consciousness. These ideas can be anything ranging from a good new insight to an old joke or a flashy phrase. Even God might speak to me in this way maybe telling me where to look for something important to my writing or even warning me to watch my words and steady up.

On the road these collapsed bodies would build up during the day when the process of stumbling drunks continues as we kept travelling and, come the evening, I would sit down on my canvas chair outside our rig, with pen and notebook, and try to harvest their meanings often by walking around them and giving them a bit of a kick and to see if they were worth sobering up.

Strange eh? Well that's writing for you; the strangest job in a strange world.

I say all this because that's how I arrived at my line about the fall of Sydney, a line which upset many of my Facebook readers who had written to tell me so since many believe, with some justification, that Sydney is nothing less than heaven on earth.

An even stranger object turned up in my gang of drunks lately and I couldn't make any sense out of it at all even though I knew it to be important and having some real and relevant meaning to something or other. It was a black rainbow just plonked down there on the floor of my mind, a metaphor telling me something about Sydney, I guessed – hence my words about the fall of Sydney. But I had no more than that.

But something important to Sydney did happen two days after my last post about the way all arms of the media had soaked the city with violence on all levels. I knew something important was going to happen to Sydney and happen it did.

***

Meet the tubby and turbulent figure of Man Horan Monis who was born Mohammed Hassan Monteghi in Iran in 1964. He was married by 21 and attained the rank of authority on Islam in religious circles. He told Australian immigration, when he first arrived, that he had fallen foul of Iran after publishing a book of subversive poetry there. Iran's secret police were always after him, he added.

He adopted an array of names after settling in Australia and early in 2001 he chained himself to the gates of the parliament in Western Australia. He began writing letters to people like UN General Secretary Kofi Anan, the BBC, the New York Times and the US President Bill Clinton. He also wrote vicious letters to the families of fallen Australian soldiers telling them their sons had died in vain.

So what we have here is yet another immaculate romantic, totally overwhelmed by himself and his own importance and unable to tell the difference between dream and reality.

In Sydney he set himself up as a clairvoyant, acquiring more than 500 clients, mainly women. In some years he managed to gross around $65,000. This business also gave him the opportunity for sexual assault and he was later charged with more than 200 offences conducted during his work. He gave himself the title Sheikh Horan.

In 2010 – after he had collapsed in the street twice – a psychiatrist diagnosed him as a schizophrenic. Later he was in debt and his attempts to gather a following had failed while he was widely rejected in the Islamic community. He was also rejected by the Hell's Angels (a group of motorcyclists, well known, we should remember, for grievous bodily harm and drug dealing) as being too weird. Monis was also alleged to have been an accessory to the murder of his first wife and was even disowned by the murderous reptiles of ISIS to whom he claimed to belong.

All Monis really stood for were the lurid, competing ideas of his chaotic mind.

***

At 8.33am on December 15, 2015 Monis walked into the Lindt Café in Martin Place in central Sydney and sat there ordering a cup of tea and a cake but otherwise saying nothing. He was carrying a sawn off shotgun in his bag and wearing a white T-shirt, black jacket and baseball cap. His choice of seat was revealing: bang opposite the huge plate glass windows of Seven Network's television newsroom where you can see the journalists and cameras from the street. As a public stage on which he was about to perform it was perfect. Here he would get maximum publicity for what he was about to do.

Monis asked to see the manager Tori Johnson and, after a brief conversation, when the staff could see something was up, Johnson told a colleague: "Everything is ok. Tell the staff to stay calm." Moments later Monis donned a bandana, taking out his shotgun and declaring to everyone there: "This is an attack. I have a bomb."

The choice of the bandana is immediately revealing. The problem with schizophrenics is generally they have no identity of their own and, in this terrifying situation, will adopt any other they might find attractive or want to identify with. The bandana is the key emblem of the Rambo character in that series of films of the same name and, in their combat dress and headgear, these shooters, particularly in American schools, are showing how closely they identify with their murderous super-hero.

A Rambo film was not showing in Sydney that week but there were plenty of others who could have fed Monis with new violent ideas and images from Brad Pitt's Fury to Mockingjay, in which people had bags put over their heads before being shot and Gone Girl in which - as I have already noted - there was the bloodiest and most prolonged stabbing you will ever see on a screen.

At gunpoint Monis made eighteen people line up against the wall and ordered them to participate in his specially made-for-television moment by telling them to stand up on benches and hold up an Islamic-type flag to the window. He hadn't even brought his own flag – and got the wrong one sent in – so we can already see he had not prepared well for his big last stand. One hostage said later he decided that Monis was just making it up as he went along since almost all his stories contradicted one another. The poor sap didn't even know how many hostages he had.

Then he asked his hostages to contact various arms of the media, telling Marcia Mikhael to issue his demands via YouTube and Facebook. Mark Burrows was told to contact Channel Nine. Most of the hostages did as they were told, many of them in tears, while few of them understood – and still don't – what he was actually demanding.

The only man who seemed to have had any real understanding of Monis' stature or importance in the community was the Moslem funeral director of North Sydney who, when asked later if he would bury him, snorted: "I might just about throw his body in the river." Then, on reflection, he added: "But no, perhaps the best place for him would be the shithouse."

***

The police had been alerted and were soon on the scene. A police terror unit had also been called and police snipers took up positions in neighbouring buildings. Local television news cameras had been on the case from the start with Channel Nine setting up on a local rooftop soon followed by five others, many of them staying there making live broadcasts with no breaks – not even for the ads - right to the end of the siege.

But by now another far more ominous gang was also gathering on the boulevard outside. These would be the foreign news cameras all come to record the doings of one mad man who didn't know what he wanted or, if he did, how to explain it and barely warranted being buried in a shithouse.

Live pictures from the scene were broadcast by CNN, the BBC, al Jazeera and other cable companies, all soon trending on the net. CNN took a live feed and the BBC put together a news feature called: "Who are Australia's radicalised Muslims?" The

Wall Street Journal and the New York Times followed up with in-depth reports from Sydney and it all even began running throughout the Spanish-speaking world of South America.

Don't think of all this as news spreading around the world: think of it more as a monsoon of black rain sweeping through every country everywhere. Think of it terrorism's finest moment so far although, as we all now know, there would be a lot, lot more to come.

***

At 2.14am, 17 hours later, Tori Johnson attacked Monis while he was dozing and Monis jumped up, later making him kneel on the floor before shooting him twice in the head. The police unit immediately made their move, blasting the café windows and letting off flash-bangs to create a diversion. Two officers fired 22 rounds, hitting Monis thirteen times in the body. Another hostage, Catrina Dawson, was killed by ricocheting police shrapnel. The siege was over.

***

So we can all see that one way or another almost all the arms of Sydney's violence-loving media may well have been involved in the Martin Place siege that day from the feature films in the local cinema to the television news services (both national and international) and, of course, the rotten video games and useless violence-loving newspapers. They all had blood on their hands; they were all as guilty as one another in - as the city coroner put it - robbing the city of her intimacy or, as the 18th century writer Alexander Pope had it, breaking a butterfly on the wheel.

The newspapers managed to pour everything they knew and didn't know all over the incident for weeks after it took place

264

including a feature writer for The Australian who wrote an absolute masterpiece of about 1,200 words on the front page – with a turn inside - the day after the event in which he exclusively revealed he had gone into the Lindt Café for a takeaway cup of coffee and *missed* the start of the siege by about half an hour. This non-story might even be the best example I know of the complete madness that overtakes the media whenever it picks up a whiff of violence. I missed the start of the siege and this is significant because …

***

Certainly Sydney took this event very hard and, when I went down to Martin Place a week or so later, I came across more flowers than they'd put out for the funeral of Princess Diana in front of Buckingham Palace. Many Sydneysiders were weeping openly, most of them doubtless believing perhaps that this shooting really would have serious consequences not only for the future security of Sydney but also in the eyes of a watching world.

I guess many would write off this siege as a local affair in which things went wrong with just three dead – one by accident - but it didn't work like that did it? It didn't work out anything like that. The consequences of the reporting of this siege were not merely high but absolutely stratospheric.

I had finished writing my own account of the siege and was drawing up a list of the possible consequences of this moment in my notebook when a sick and out-of-control media had run up against a lone madman when, for some reason, I began wandering around my room of comatose drunks looking for a bit of inspiration and I came across that black rainbow still sitting there. The black rainbow. Mmm. A useful metaphor this. The black rainbows of death. A wonderful image for sure – something like the black rain perhaps - but what did it tell us? I gave it a kick and knew.

It told us that, far from being a local spat, this incident in Martin Place had sent black rainbows of death shooting all over the world promoting violence and death wherever they touched down. Put another way: these black rainbows rose up out of Martin Place, with the special and crucial help of all those television cameras, and, within a few weeks, provoked the massacre of the Charlie Hebdo magazine in Paris, botched gun attacks in Belgium, another gun attack in Copenhagen and sundry solo attacks in Holland and South America.

There was even a 24-hour gun battle between a lone Muslim and the police in Denmark after he had declared a personal war against what was once known as the happiest country in the world. Whether they liked it or not – and whether they wanted it to happen or not – this sick media had made bombing and shooting a global fashion in which slumbering psychos and schizophrenics everywhere decided they wanted to take part. The media massed here in Martin Place had sent out a wake-up call throughout the world promising everyone they too could achieve global prominence and announce their immortal presence to the world if only they took a leaf out of Monis's book.

You don't believe me?

Why else do you think so many of our major cities all over the world have been locked in so much street riot and anarchy for so long in recent years? Why do the figures on our school massacres keep rising? And why were all those seemingly stable governments brought down in the Middle East so fast leading, as I write, to boatloads of refugees escaping from north Africa looking for safety and stability for themselves and their families, huge numbers of them drowning, with their children, in the Mediterranean as they did so?

It was all because the world had been watching the same television news with its fast-moving narratives and violent imagery. That's all it is. You really don't have to look anywhere else even if everyone always does, particularly our wretched media. Television and newspapers have become the main agents of lawlessness in our modern world and they get away with everything – even the finger of suspicion pointed at them - often putting the blame for all this gusting anarchy on the social media which, one body of research found, had nothing to do with it.

And they are absolutely brilliant at justifying their every move, doubtless ready to point out that they could hardly have given Monis an intelligence or sanity test before they set up their huge reporting machine around the Lindt café. No, they could not, but, when they see a man go into a café, threatening to blow up everyone with a bomb he didn't even have, they could have safely assumed – or at least strongly suspected - he was a total nutcase and trod very carefully before making this nutcase not only significant but a huge and influential figure, who would also become world famous, a standing which would certainly have figured highly in his early calculations when he was planning his attack.

The other grave and obvious fault of the media in such affairs, of course, is that it always needs to characterise these nitwits as holy warriors because it somehow suits their agenda to paint an apocalyptic portrait of them as coming for us from out of the desert with a machete in one hand and the Koran in the other. But nothing could be further from the truth with all of them. Most of them are simply nuts.

Monis belonged to no group – not even the Hells Angels would have him – and in another incident around that period a shooter actually said that he was looking for the fame that he knew the media would give him.

I was quietly satisfied with my writing on the siege. Theological journalism I had called it in another life: the way I had found what I believed to be real facts and married them to the insights which I also believed had come from my Malaysian visions. But the truly interesting aspect of this theological journalism, particularly here in Australia, I thought, was that a lot of other people got it too. A quarter of a million had got it and I was no longer a lone prophet ranting in his battered online pulpit to rows of empty pews.

I had conflated two of my reports on the siege into what you have just read and Facebookers had given my first post about the siege a total of around 200,000 visits, with 3,000 likes and a staggering 1,431 shares. Then there was a second attack on the media: The Black Rainbows of Death which brought in 179,520 visits with 1,429 shares.

I didn't know who or where they all these people were, of course, but I had paid to promote those posts to direct them into Australia so, with the 1,431 shares, which could come to almost anything because a share is something you send on to your friends, who may well send them on to their own friends elsewhere, my analysis of the siege could even have been read by well over half a million.

These figures are not exactly Justin Bieber standards, I know, and I'm not claiming that all those who read them believed what I wrote, but I do claim I had clearly spoken to the minds of these people – mostly Australians – and indeed crystallised their own thoughts about their own media. They had shown me that they too shared my grave reservations about what this diseased media of theirs was actually doing to this sacred country and indeed to the world.

And what did the Australian media do? Erm ... well nothing. It certainly didn't even indulge in the faintest bout of self-examination, remaining too busy writing about the ISIS "threat". ISIS Ready To Take Over Australia was one later unsubstantiated headline a few days later in The Australian newspaper. My old editor on The Sunday Times, the revered Harold Evans, would have gone absolutely mental scrawling "Evidence?" over the proofs of such stories or else simply spiking them.

And what did the politicians do or say? Erm... again nothing. They were all too busy tap dancing in front of the media - hoping for any favourable coverage - to even dare saying anything at all critical about it. Premier Tony Abbott said: "This incident echoed around the world. Tens if not millions of people have been focussed on Sydney which has been touched by terrorism for the first time in more than 35 years."

So how and in what way did this incident echo right round the world Tony? Who, with its gross exaggerations, deep confusions and downright lies, did it? Did this news spread by homing pigeons or letters or semaphore or even phone calls home? Of course not. This news was spread around the world mainly by television cameras aided by newspapers, which also had dire consequences for Muslim communities everywhere with many suffering from hate attacks by children as young as ten, in the UK according to one later report by Teeside University, although most of the perpetrators were identified as being over 40.

Noticeable spikes in attacks took place throughout the world immediately after the Sydney siege, the same report found, and these attacks included online abuse to threats, street-based assaults and extreme violence. Most of the UK attacks took place on women wearing distinctive Muslim clothing. Another similar spike happened after the death of Drummer Lee Rigby on May 22, 2013 where, as we have already noted in an earlier chapter, the judge who presided over the trial of the two killers said the whole attack had clearly been got up for the benefit of the media.

I'm not even sure any Canberra politician has ever asked one penetrating question about the media and the way it clearly feeds and controls terror and themselves. But if one politician ever did stand up against the Australian media who would report what they said? All that would happen is that this brave politician would acquire a powerful enemy who would either set out to destroy him or, more likely, just ignore him altogether.

This is a real global tyranny we face here which is poisoning every home and mind and I want to tell Australia in particular, whose own media has contributed greatly, if not actually started, this current global storm in Sydney, that God wants this attack to stop.

Such words may raise the spectre of censorship but these storms of madness, which are driving the world crazy and look like growing, particularly in America, until barely anyone is left standing, are way beyond the influence and power of any would-be censor. And all these storms need to keep going are the idiots who now see a machete as the new fashion item. All they need to become motivated and guided is a supine and sick media which has set up this long and seemingly never-ending age of black rain.

No, censorship simply could not work although this sorry and growing mess – which seems to get worse almost every hour - tells me the world is moving into end times when God is preparing to pour out his spirit all over the world and, in such days, your sons and daughters will prophecy, your young men shall see visions and your old men dream dreams.

But there is good news: oh yes there is hot good news straight up from the mountains of North Wales and the news is that God still loves and cares for us all whether we be black, brown or white. He also wants it known, as a matter of the gravest urgency, that unless this deeply romantic tyranny falls, everything and everyone you have ever loved will fall too.

Oh yes, unless the world finds a way of bringing this long season of black rain to an end he wants it known - and fully understood – that all your sunsets are going to be full of his heartbreak and all your fields will become barren and dry and all your harvests and all your rainbows will be black and dead.

44: Be Ready for the Second Coming

As our journey through Oz came to an end Liz was getting quite weepy about leaving this fabulous country saying, repeatedly, that it had given her the best year of her life and she couldn't even remember one bad moment in it. Well I wasn't quite with her on that and certainly remember quite a few bad moments with that nutty lizard forever trying to escape in the Blue Mountains, that tyre blow-out on the Nullarbor and that blow-fish who kept eating people's toes in Coral Bay.

But you remember what you want to remember, I guess.

She was still crying in front of the immigration official on our Sydney departure as we were about to get on the Aurora, our ship home, and the official clearly thought she was crying in shame because we had overstayed our visa by ten days. But that wasn't the case at all. We had certainly overstayed our visa but she was crying because she was leaving Australia. Yet those tears worked out well for us because they merely chastised us mildly for our overstay as she appeared to be so genuinely and tearfully sorry we had broken their rules.

But the same official told us later that had we overstayed by 28 days we would have been banned from Australia for three years. Three years!

***

What had made our departure harder to take was that our final few weeks there had been spent in another paradise with the eye of the sun.

Again courtesy of Happy House Sitters, we had been living as the sole occupants of Wirral Grange near Cessnock which had four bedrooms, a swimming pool and an orchard, and set in its own vineyard. Two cleaners came in twice a week and we had a full-blown zoo as a next door neighbour which had a koala who clung to a pole when they wanted to take him out to meet visitors and flatly refused to let go. We were also surrounded by the thousands of acres of vineyards in the marvellous Hunter Valley.

The owners of the Grange, Carol and Terry Hughes, who ran their book distribution business from there, had gone to a conference in New Zealand and had left us the keys to the office ute AND their wine cellar. But we didn't drink one drop of that wine your honour. In the old days as a Fleet Street hack I might even have sat in that cellar and had a fair go at drinking myself to death. But not any more and certainly not after New Norcia. The painful hangovers in the mornings were never worth the doubtful pleasure of becoming more and more comatose the night before, I had long decided, even if I knew that sobriety was an extremely fragile possession, quickly lost in the ever welcoming quicksands of my addiction.

Our sole responsibility in the Grange was to look after two friendly collie dogs, Brandy and Remy, feed a dozen chickens first thing and, every other day, a grumpy horse out in his own meadow who didn't like anyone mounting him. At least there were no nutty lizards to keep banged up.

The surrounding vineyards spoke to me on many levels, particularly with my much-replenished faith after travelling through Australia. What I enjoyed doing there at night was to sit outside the back door of the Grange beneath a night of stars and look up. A shooting star might go past and then another and another. These shooting stars always seemed far brighter than normal stars and bigger and closer. An angel hurrying about its duties, I often thought, taking a message to the other side of the kingdom. This angel might even be carrying the time and date of the Second Coming, a secret thus far locked in the heart of the Father.

On such star-studded nights I also marvelled at the perfect balance of the universe; how everything seems to be propped up by huge, if invisible, scaffolding and how this balance, in turn, reflected the balance of God himself. But, closer to the ground, I also loved to walk in the vineyards themselves, taking a handful of grapes perhaps and squeezing them hard, making my fingers bleed with luxuriant blood, giving me an insight into why wine is as potent as bread in religion; why there is always the imagery of red wine in serious, devoted societies.

Yes, my faith had certainly got into good shape and there were regular prayers out here in Australia. My first indication I was really making some progress along the rock-strewn path of a modern faith came with my post Why God Wants the Media to Lay Down Its Arms which pulled in, within a couple of days, 210 shares, 539 likes with a reach of 23,488 on a promotion of £63. This was a real breakthrough for me particularly as I had been writing a lot about God in my earlier books, a subject which I would never claim had ever generated a lot of interest. Or sales come to that.

A Savage Pilgrimage Beneath a Blood Red Moon achieved 15,000 visits on another promotion of £63. Then there was Cyclones, Fires and Locusts as the Language of God which had a reach of 106,080 with 61 shares and 1,167 likes on a promotion of £130.

Then, of course, the The Black Rainbows of Death Now Circling the World which, along with my other attack on the media brought in more than a quarter of a million.

Oh that last one was such a surprise. Yes, I WAS NOT ALONE.

Trialling my stuff on Facebook might even have been the best move I'd made since starting as a writer some thirty years ago. I had cut and even eliminated poorly received posts confidently - according to what the figures were telling me - and what is more began writing about themes that I had earlier decided I wouldn't touch because people weren't interested in them. But the Aussies were interested in God, I now saw. It was merely because no one was telling them anything about God, I guessed, and they were perhaps taking a lot of their ideas from this doomed media of theirs which, out here anyway, was as godless as it was useless and destructive.

These figures finally gave me the credibility I hadn't had before; they made my ideas more than my personal testimony; they gave me a quarter of a million reasons why I could talk to the disenfranchised Facebook generation about God: young people who didn't anyway want access to the normal media where they often told you how to think and how to live.

My quarter of a million had all bobbed up on my page saying yes, yes, yes. This media is obsessed by violence, cruelty and terror, they revel in murder and sexual inconstancy and, in everything they do and say, they are sick and should be put down.

It wouldn't be quite so bad if those who ran and wrote for the media weren't all so self-important and self-righteous, convinced their stories were actually saving the world when, with almost every word they wrote or image they presented, our poor world got far,

far worse. And these reports had led to spikes in violence everywhere, not just Australia, not only causing death and pain to those immediately involved but sentencing whole families and friends the world over to lifetimes of loss and pain from which they would never recover.

Yet the greatest significance of my figures, for me, was that they now gave me the confidence to be bold, to go deep and to tell people things about God. Such figures, of course, might not have been enough to satisfy the sternest theologian but they sure as hell satisfied me; telling me my somewhat rocky career as a freelance prophet might not be the complete failure that it had so often appeared. If nothing else those figures gave me a good start or it might even turn out they gave me a mighty fine end.

***

I believe God took hold of our journey around Australia right from the beginning, always watching out for our safety and getting us back to Sydney just in time for the siege so that I could then report on who and what was behind it and the unimaginable consequences for the world which issued out of it. God loved and trusted me enough to get me back to Sydney to bear witness to the total mess – that package of the blackest lies – this sick media had put together in Martin Place.

I suspected very early on that God was active in our lives particularly as we hadn't first sailed to Australia to make a journey around this country. We had come here with enough money and a plan to set up Nathan in an art gallery in Sydney much like our own which we had been running successfully for the past ten years back home in Bala in the mountains of North Wales. We had the money to set up this new Sydney business and decided that we would take a year to find suitable premises and import originals and prints from the UK which we would sell to the Australians who all seemed to have ancestral connections with the UK in some way or other, even if there were some connections they might not want to talk about or remember. I had a good title for our new gallery too: Pom Art.

But Nathan had decided he wanted to start his own signage business so that was Pom Art straight down the drain leaving us with a visa for a year together with a pile of money so it was only then that we decided on our tour through the Bush. It wasn't even until we bought our Winnebago and sorted out its many problems that we took off up the road north of Sydney with no plan at all except a vague one to follow that road.

I'm not even sure we would have left Wales had we known what was before us. As I mentioned at the start of this book I'd had a few operations in recent years which had left me pretty weak and this wretched plantar fasciitis was not only paining my foot particularly first thing in the morning – and still does - but meant that Liz would have to drive every mile of the way. But she was happy enough about that and never once complained.

Indeed I was bit of a wreck, to say the least, but, as I now see it, God had got us both to Australia then opened the door to our road trip and pushed us through it, propping us up and holding us steady whenever we staggered. I still believe he looked after us when that tree came crashing down next to us in our rig in that storm in Sydney, just missing us by inches. Had that tree hit us there would have been no trip anywhere.

Liz didn't see it in the same way however; where I always saw the hand of God, she believed we had just been lucky. But we simply had so much more going for us that the success of the trip – including selling the Winnebago the day before we sailed home for almost as much as we paid for it – surely could not have been down to mere luck. There had to be a lot more than that at work.

People who have known me all my life often said that I must have been very lucky to have travelled so much and so far particularly from an early age when I went off abroad almost annually. But again I don't think that was luck or indeed any part of it. God always looked after me from a very early age and kept opening doors for me because he wanted me to see the world for myself and not through the eyes of others. He wanted me to know what I was writing about and becoming a well-travelled columnist for newspapers helped in that too, because I met and interviewed every important film-maker and writer who came to London in that period.

As a columnist, particularly when I was on the Observer, I could practically go to any part of the world I fancied. My bosses never seemed to care where I went – and always first class – as long as they got their copy on time for next Sunday's edition. I'd had a good run on The Observer and reader research had found that there were two main features in the paper which held their circulation together: Clive James' television reviews and my Pendennis column.

Indeed I was always popping back and for to Israel – where they always took their press relations very seriously – and once landed there to be met by a limo with my own personal driver on the tarmac. I even had my own bicycle parked in the Garden Tomb there and was thinking that Jerusalem was going to be an important staging post in my spiritual journey even if that turned out not to be true. The real and most significant staging post for me – as it turned out - was Australia.

In a long and wandering life to all corners of the world the Australian people seemed to be the first to actually listen to what I was trying to tell them. How they have been saddled with the image of grog-swilling, foul-mouthed baboons I can never imagine since, almost to a man, I have found them to be intelligent, discerning souls, born to surf high waves in the sun and interested in any new ideas that might be put in front of them.

In my homeland all my ideas have usually been greeted by rejection. I even made a film about what was going on in Northern Ireland and why. It was due to be shown throughout the UK but pulled at the last minute in Northern Ireland because they clearly feared its impact. They know my ideas could kill them simply because they are the truth.

I also wouldn't have been at all surprised if God also had something to do with messing up my attempted drug-taking in Nimbin. He does like me drug-free and sober, that's for sure. He likes me clean because I think and write better that way. You're never any use to anyone when you're falling down drunk or stoned out of your brain. All the early bad periods in my marriage coincided with long spells of drinking or drug-taking.

Most of my books have reflected my lifelong struggle with God which had begun in Malaysia and, as they had hardly taken over the charts, I was sure that, this time, with the Grey Nomads, I really did have an entertaining and lively subject which would do well. This seemed to be a real story about real people who were clearly changing Australia and themselves at the end of their lives. Oh yes, all that added up to a good story for sure and I'm not at all certain why I finally moved away from the nomads and was again more drawn to God and that, even early in this journey I had begun feeling his presence quite strongly.

Although, on reflection, he again must have had a lot to do with that.

When we returned to Britain and I had finished this book there was also the age-old problem for any writer of where to get it published. A few letters I had sent to publishers - even those who had once published me – went unanswered and a London agent I had been using hadn't read it either after I had sent it to him. A month or so later it emerged that not only had he still not read it he didn't even know where it was although I had a signed receipt that it had at least landed in his office.

So perhaps God wasn't looking after me after all as I had earlier imagined and I was even thinking of packing it all in when I sent an email describing the contents of this book to Chris Jones of Cambria Books in west Wales. He responded enthusiastically and immediately saying that, after he read it he would certainly do it as an ebook and as a printed book. When I sent him the disc he again responded on the same day saying it would be an "honour" to publish this book and offered me a contract saying they might even be able to get it all out within a few weeks. Phew! Any writer will tell you that it normally takes at least a year for a book to work its way through the system. And improbable that any publisher would be "honoured" to do so.

Perhaps I really was being looked after because the transition from writing the first page to publication had been seamless and almost totally free of hiccups. I don't know how this book will be received, of course, but I'd finally told my story to the best of my ability and got it out That's all that seemed to matter.

***

But I sort of had a quiet confidence it would do well, particularly because of how the Facebook figures had kept mounting dizzyingly as I wrote it and I knew that, in that incomprehensible and unpredictable way of his, God had got hold of me again and was opening a new door for me and was not about to let go.

But then everything changed for me and, as the Facebook figures kept mounting dizzyingly, I knew that, in that incomprehensible and unpredictable way of his, he had got hold of me again and was not about to let go.

Yes, he had appointed me as one of his prophets whether I liked it or not, and I was going to tell the world what he wanted the world to hear, whether I approved of it or not and whatever disappointment I might have had with the sales of my books about him had nothing to do with it. I had been saddled with a job for life and I would get my final reward elsewhere. So get on with it. A vision was a vision and I couldn't just forget about it because it had become inconvenient or I wanted to write a funny book or make money.

But the Biblical prophets were all strange, mad people, I had to keep reassuring myself. One lived in a cave and another with a prostitute. And their one other common feature was that they were all reluctant; they all wanted to do something else.

***

So the end had finally come in the Hunter Valley and I was staring out at another storm raging over the vineyards happy, at last, that I had finally managed to finish my story here in an Australian vineyard which had started so tumultuously more than fifty years ago in the paddy fields of north Malaysia.

Not that the media were showing any signs of calming down. ISIS had recently started blowing up temples and putting out videos of their grim work on the net. And what do you know but even the BBC – along with the rest of the world's television new services - were putting this "news" out on their bulletins together with the ISIS videos.

What message does all this give to the rest of the world? I will tell you. It tells you that if you manage to blow up something big and important or if you can manage to mow down 80 people while they are sunbathing in Tunisia or if you can destroy a holy museum then you are absolutely guaranteed a big spot on the news together with an appropriate examination of your motives and many follow-up features in which they will also interview your relatives and anyone else who may have known you for five minutes when you were young and spotty.

***

We didn't do much in our few weeks in Wirral Grange as it happened, just lay around reading or watching tennis on television. We swam in the pool and I wrote a fair bit as I have done every day, for three hours, for the last thirty years including Sundays. I now had a lot to write about but I never wrote more than the three hours a day; always made sure never to make myself tired. If you do get tired all that happens is that you make the tiredness worse and soon stop writing anything. I am sure that's why so many wannabees give up writing so early and easily. They simply don't understand what a long, nit-picking process writing a book is and, failing to enjoy that slow nit-picking process, often end up in a hurry, spoiling it all and just giving up.

Yet I hadn't ever dreamed my story would have a proper end and couldn't imagine what a proper end might be. I always feared my work would be a bit of a puzzle to many who read it; the ravings of a writer who'd had a strange experience in a Malaysian paddy field, perhaps, and who kept trying to make of it what wasn't there.

So now my story really had come to a full stop and, wiping a tear from my eye, I knew it was all over for me as a writer and perhaps I'd have to find something else to while away my last few years.

But maybe God has other plans for me. He is first and last his own man and you simply never know what he's going to do next.

***

We are a rational people, by and large, and I am convinced that issues such as terrorism could be solved by the application of cold rationality and that we could easily set out to tell the media that what it is doing is not rational; that it is time for all this reporting of carnage to stop and, like it or not, believe it or not, the media is playing an absolutely crucial role in the fertilisation and growth of modern terrorism and mass shootings which are growing everywhere and have become a plague in America.

The people who do set out to say something about the media are almost always woeful and clueless. One police half-wit, after a particularly bad shooting in an Oregon school, said that he would never use the shooter's name because he had plainly been seeking publicity all along. There might be an element of truth in what the policeman was saying except the shooter shot himself dead after the event, as so many do, so he would hardly have been able to enjoy the fame which his act had brought him.

The local media monkeys clearly had no such misgivings about naming the shooter and quickly interviewed the father and even published the dead son's manifesto in full. They always seem to be so sublimely unaware that they have anything at all to do with the growth of terrorism. They are our friends, always doing an important job, here to help.

President Obama, yet again, did his famous imitation of a bad hiccup ranting about gun control and it was clear that all these intelligent men, these so-called experts, just could not see the wood for the trees.

All these shooters are the diseased offspring of a diseased media and I am not here referring specifically to the world of film and television, video games or newspapers but to all of them, particularly the news industry. They all brought attention to these atrocities in the first place and spattered it over every home in the name of keeping us all informed about what's going on. "When he comes he will come with all the powers and miracles of the lie," says the Bible.

Thus the black rain keeps pouring down on us all, seeking the sick and out-of-control to work with and setting up the iron laws of fashion which very few can resist. All that we can really know for certain is that, whatever Obama might tell us, these shootings will continue, because there is not one person in any position of authority who seems to understand why people are pulling their triggers in the first place.

Except me who, it has to be admitted, did have an excellent and totally reliable witness from the beginning.

**

I've just finished reading an extract from a book by Jason Burke, The New Threat From Islamic Militancy, in the Guardian. Burke is clearly extremely intelligent and a fine writer who sets out the whos, whys and whats of Isis terrorism. He points out that death by terrorists in the UK is relatively low, particularly when set against the carnage throughout the Middle East – it is 55 in the UK in fact – but even news of this small number fills us with fear: terrorism always achieves it success by the news of the destruction they make rather than the actual violence they commit, he writes. Thus, after an attack, we all feel a pang of fear after learning where and how the attack may have taken place. This is how terrorism works and why it has become so frightening for all of us.

Yes, fine, good, but why doesn't Burke also explain how news of even relatively unimportant carnage fills us all with fear? Why can't he explain and spell out why terrorists always use – and need – the massive syringe of a 24-hour news media to inject us all with terrorist poison and fill us all full of fear?

No media, no fear. That's the crucial bit that all commentators on terrorism always leave out. Surely it couldn't be because all our commentators on terrorism work for the media? Could it?

This is certainly why our media's hold over all communications everywhere is so tyrannical and supreme. If you want to say anything at all to anyone anywhere you just have to use it – and your words always have to be somehow sanctioned by it - and the penalties for not being so sanctioned can be very high indeed. I am the luckiest ever writer to have found someone as brave as Chris Jones of Cambria Books.

Certainly the media's big bugs are always ready to defend its honour blindly and ferociously. I did once appear on BBC Radio's Moral Maze with six or so top journos sitting around the table and when I sat at the head of the table, as a guest, opposite the chair Michael Buerk, an old friend from my days on the Western Mail, I announced that it was clear to me, if no one else, that the media was – and always had been – firmly behind the Troubles in Northern Ireland. "It's not violence in Northern Ireland that's the problem but the media's pursuit of it," I continued.

I shall never forget the sight of all of them, with their arses a good six inches off their chairs, shouting at me at the same time. Many were making such strangulated sounds I could barely understand what they were saying and I suppose it's worth pointing out that, as far as I knew, not one of them had ever been to Belfast and covered events in Northern Ireland as I once had, albeit briefly and badly.

I had on occasion offered my views on the media in the Observer – and even God's views on it – and there might have been a quick meeting of the newspaper's top executives to discuss if the column should be used. "But the force and depth of my ideas were clear and it was, of course, always beautifully written," Donald Trelford, then editor of the Observer, told Central Television who had made a film about me thanks to the courage of director John Whatmore. "So we let it go."

But if they were alarmed by my column when it was written they calmed down when they got our readers' response to it which was always phenomenal. "You will never write so much in so few words for as long as you live," a former BBC executive wrote to me after, one Easter, I had written about the possibility of ever again seeing a revival in this country in our lifetime, "a revival which have to break through the media's power over our lives."

So I guess I was never really crying alone in the wilderness and God was looking after me when I did make any sort of breakthrough on his behalf. I could indeed make contact with many serious people who agreed with me although, of course, I had to use the media to do so. If you ever want the world to listen to anything you say then you must always use the media, an insight which all terrorists have grasped so clearly and firmly.

When people in the free world question whether terrorism would stop if it was no longer reported I would ask another question. The real question surely is: if the free world allows such reportage to continue, will it remain free? Is the price of freedom a world full of killing, bombing and fear? Because that's exactly where the media is taking us: straight into a world where terrorism is going to keep growing simply because terrorists know exactly how to manipulate a violence-loving, irrational media while we don't know - and fail to understand - what makes and grows terrorism in the first place.

The routine justification the media rolls out for doing what it does is that their reportage prevents governments working in secret and dispels rumour. But if that's the sole justification for what they do they could report all terrorist incidents factually in a few paragraphs way down on an inside page. That would cover the problems with government secrecy and dispelling rumour.

But they would never do that since their reports would then lose all drama, impact and terror, which terrorists are looking for. Anyway, despite what it might ever say to the contrary, the media is not slightly interested in making the world a better place: all the print media wants is to sell newspapers and make money. That's the clear, unwritten rule behind everything they do and why they will always be prone to writing inaccurate and often totally imaginary reports about the next gang of hairy-arsed terrorists due to come wandering down the mountain, Kalashnikov in one hand and scrapbook with their press cuttings in the other.

***

And as we are asking questions let's ask – and answer – a few more. If we never heard another word about terrorists what would we lose?

Nothing.

And what would the terrorists lose if not another word was written about them?

Everything.

They would lose everything they need to grow and prosper in a world which barely seems to understand how they got so big and terrifying in the first place.

***

But there is another deeper and far more exciting prospect before us which is this: what we are seeing, in the rise of the modern media, as it takes over the world, was foreseen in every aspect and detail in the Bible. In our lives we have seen the rise and rise of the Man of Lawlessness and, as I have already explained, this great tide of evil, the Bible says, will be ruthlessly exposed in its own season.

So my final message from the Hunter Valley on my Welsh online pulpit is this: Be prepared, my beloved Aussies, since sometime soon - and perhaps sooner than any of you might ever expect – this evil and deeply romantic tyranny will be firmly and finally repulsed by the transcendental brilliance of the Second Coming and, when he comes, he will destroy this evil just with the words out of his mouth.

One step in the Bush, that's all it's going to take to begin freeing our imprisoned world from its terror and fear.

Just one step.

Now concerning the coming of our Lord Jesus Christ and our assembling to meet him, we beg you, brethren, not to be quickly shaken in mind or excited, either by spirit or word, or by letter purporting to be from us, to the effect that the day of the Lord has come. Let no one deceive you in any way; for that day will not come, unless the rebellion comes first and the man of lawlessness is revealed, the son of perdition (2 Thess. 2: 1-3 RSV)

Lightning Source UK Ltd.
Milton Keynes UK
UKOW01f1957071115

262245UK00001B/8/P